D1827131

Identity Federation
Complete Self-Assessment Guide

The guidance in this Self-Assessment is based on Identity Federation best practices and standards in business process architecture, design and quality management. The guidance is also based on the professional judgment of the individual collaborators listed in the Acknowledgments.

Notice of rights

You are licensed to use the Self-Assessment contents in your presentations and materials for internal use and customers without asking us - we are here to help.

Trademarks

Many of the designations used by manufacturers and sellers to distinguish their products are claimed as trademarks. Where those designations appear in this book, and the publisher was aware of a trademark claim, the designations appear as requested by the owner of the trademark. All other product names and services identified throughout this book are used in editorial fashion only and for the benefit of such companies with no intention of infringement of the trademark. No such use, or the use of any trade name, is intended to convey endorsement or other affiliation with this book.

Table of Contents

About The Art of Service

The Art of Service, Business Process Architects since 2000, is dedicated to helping stakeholders achieve excellence.

Defining, designing, creating, and implementing a process to solve a stakeholders challenge or meet an objective is the most valuable role… In EVERY group, company, organization and department.

Unless you're talking a one-time, single-use project, there should be a process. Whether that process is managed and implemented by humans, AI, or a combination of the two, it needs to be designed by someone with a complex enough perspective to ask the right questions.

Someone capable of asking the right questions and step back and say, 'What are we really trying to accomplish here? And is there a different way to look at it?'

With The Art of Service's Standard Requirements Self-Assessments, we empower people who can do just that — whether their title is marketer, entrepreneur, manager, salesperson, consultant, Business Process Manager, executive assistant, IT Manager, CIO etc... —they are the people who rule the future. They are people who watch the process as it happens, and ask the right questions to make the process work better.

Contact us when you need any support with this Self-Assessment and any help with templates, blue-prints and examples of standard documents you might need:

http://theartofservice.com
service@theartofservice.com

Included Resources - how to access

Included with your purchase of the book is the Identity

Federation Self-Assessment Spreadsheet Dashboard which contains all questions and Self-Assessment areas and auto-generates insights, graphs, and project RACI planning - all with examples to get you started right away.

How? Simply send an email to
access@theartofservice.com
with this books' title in the subject to get the Identity Federation Self Assessment Tool right away.

You will receive the following contents with New and Updated specific criteria:

- The latest quick edition of the book in PDF

- The latest complete edition of the book in PDF, which criteria correspond to the criteria in...

- The Self-Assessment Excel Dashboard, and...

- Example pre-filled Self-Assessment Excel Dashboard to get familiar with results generation

- In-depth specific Checklists covering the topic

- Project management checklists and templates to assist with implementation

INCLUDES LIFETIME SELF ASSESSMENT UPDATES

Every self assessment comes with Lifetime Updates and Lifetime Free Updated Books. Lifetime Updates is an industry-first feature which allows you to receive verified self assessment updates, ensuring you always have the most accurate information at your fingertips.

Get it now- you will be glad you did - do it now, before you forget.

Send an email to **access@theartofservice.com** with this books' title in the subject to get the Identity Federation Self Assessment Tool right away.

Purpose of this Self-Assessment

This Self-Assessment has been developed to improve understanding of the requirements and elements of Identity Federation, based on best practices and standards in business process architecture, design and quality management.

It is designed to allow for a rapid Self-Assessment to determine how closely existing management practices and procedures correspond to the elements of the Self-Assessment.

The criteria of requirements and elements of Identity Federation have been rephrased in the format of a Self-Assessment questionnaire, with a seven-criterion scoring system, as explained in this document.

In this format, even with limited background knowledge of Identity Federation, a manager can quickly review existing operations to determine how they measure up to the standards. This in turn can serve as the starting point of a 'gap analysis' to identify management tools or system elements that might usefully be implemented in the organization to help improve overall performance.

How to use the Self-Assessment

On the following pages are a series of questions to identify to what extent your Identity Federation initiative is complete in comparison to the requirements set in standards.

To facilitate answering the questions, there is a space in front of each question to enter a score on a scale of '1' to '5'.

1 Strongly Disagree

2 Disagree

3 Neutral

4 Agree

5 Strongly Agree

Read the question and rate it with the following in front of mind:

'In my belief,
the answer to this question is clearly defined'.

There are two ways in which you can choose to interpret this statement;
1. how aware are you that the answer to the question is clearly defined
2. for more in-depth analysis you can choose to gather evidence and confirm the answer to the question. This obviously will take more time, most Self-Assessment users opt for the first way to interpret the question and dig deeper later on based on the outcome of the overall Self-Assessment.

A score of '1' would mean that the answer is not clear at all, where a '5' would mean the answer is crystal clear and defined. Leave emtpy when the question is not applicable or you don't want to answer it, you can skip it without affecting your score. Write your score in the space provided.

After you have responded to all the appropriate statements in each section, compute your average score for that section, using the formula provided, and round to the nearest tenth. Then transfer to the corresponding spoke in the Identity Federation Scorecard on the second next page of the Self-Assessment.

Your completed Identity Federation Scorecard will give you a clear presentation of which Identity Federation areas need attention.

Identity Federation Scorecard Example

Example of how the finalized Scorecard can look like:

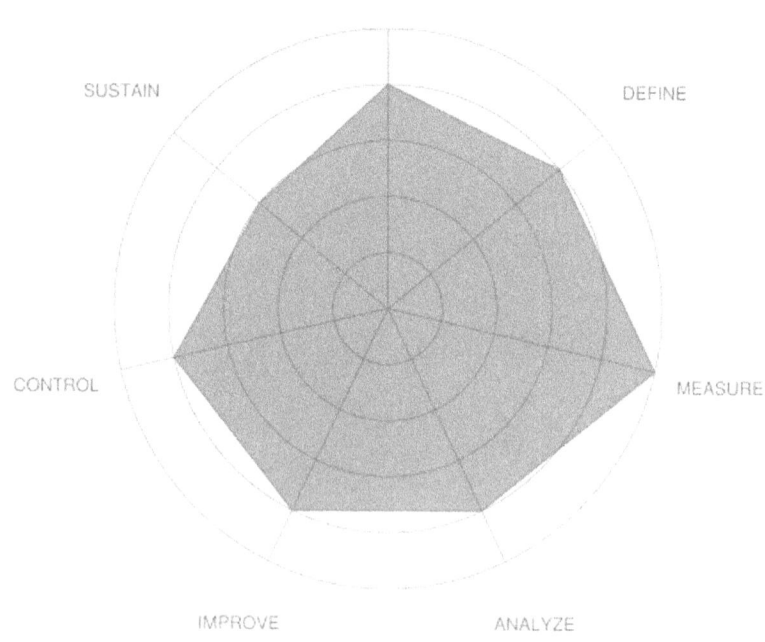

Identity Federation Scorecard

Your Scores:

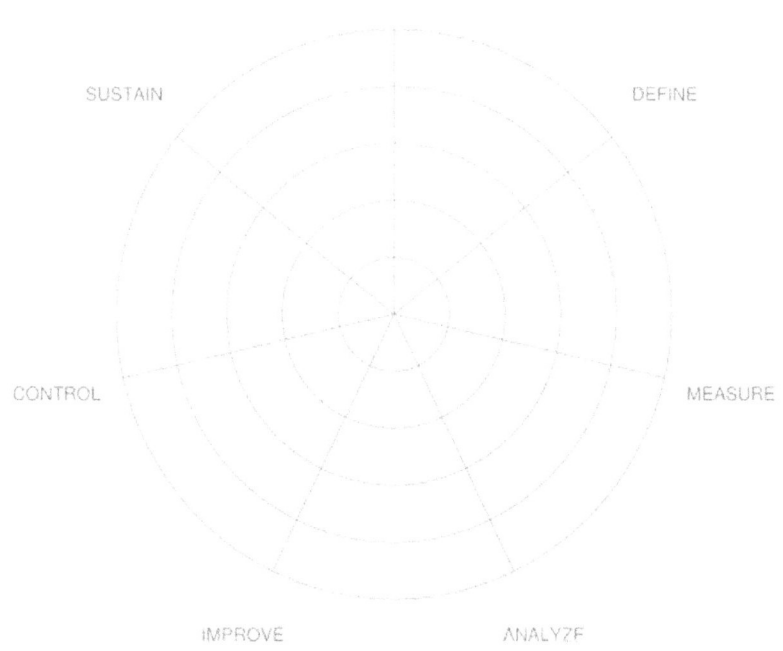

BEGINNING OF THE SELF-ASSESSMENT:

CRITERION #1: RECOGNIZE

INTENT: Be aware of the need for change. Recognize that there is an unfavorable variation, problem or symptom.

In my belief, the answer to this question is clearly defined:

5 Strongly Agree

4 Agree

3 Neutral

2 Disagree

1 Strongly Disagree

1. Who needs to know about identity federation?
<--- Score

2. Why the need?
<--- Score

3. Do you know what you need to know about identity federation?
<--- Score

4. Would you recognize a threat from the inside?
<--- Score

5. Will a response program recognize when a crisis occurs and provide some level of response?
<--- Score

6. What is the problem or issue?
<--- Score

7. Are losses recognized in a timely manner?
<--- Score

8. What do you need to start doing?
<--- Score

9. Have you identified your identity federation key performance indicators?
<--- Score

10. Where is training needed?
<--- Score

11. How are training requirements identified?
<--- Score

12. Does identity federation create potential expectations in other areas that need to be recognized and considered?
<--- Score

13. How do you recognize an objection?
<--- Score

14. Do you recognize identity federation

achievements?
<--- Score

15. Can management personnel recognize the monetary benefit of identity federation?
<--- Score

16. Do you need to avoid or amend any identity federation activities?
<--- Score

17. What should be considered when identifying available resources, constraints, and deadlines?
<--- Score

18. When a identity federation manager recognizes a problem, what options are available?
<--- Score

19. Are there recognized identity federation problems?
<--- Score

20. What is the smallest subset of the problem you can usefully solve?
<--- Score

21. Are there identity federation problems defined?
<--- Score

22. What would happen if identity federation weren't done?
<--- Score

23. Are your goals realistic? Do you need to redefine your problem? Perhaps the problem has changed or

maybe you have reached your goal and need to set a new one?
<--- Score

24. What creative shifts do you need to take?
<--- Score

25. What training and capacity building actions are needed to implement proposed reforms?
<--- Score

26. What does identity federation success mean to the stakeholders?
<--- Score

27. What situation(s) led to this identity federation Self Assessment?
<--- Score

28. Who are your key stakeholders who need to sign off?
<--- Score

29. What extra resources will you need?
<--- Score

30. What identity federation capabilities do you need?
<--- Score

31. What are the timeframes required to resolve each of the issues/problems?
<--- Score

32. How do you identify the kinds of information that you will need?
<--- Score

33. Does the problem have ethical dimensions?
<--- Score

34. What are the stakeholder objectives to be achieved with identity federation?
<--- Score

35. Are there any revenue recognition issues?
<--- Score

36. What do employees need in the short term?
<--- Score

37. What are your needs in relation to identity federation skills, labor, equipment, and markets?
<--- Score

38. What prevents you from making the changes you know will make you a more effective identity federation leader?
<--- Score

39. Are you dealing with any of the same issues today as yesterday? What can you do about this?
<--- Score

40. What are the expected benefits of identity federation to the stakeholder?
<--- Score

41. What identity federation problem should be solved?
<--- Score

42. What activities does the governance board

need to consider?
<--- Score

43. Who should resolve the identity federation issues?
<--- Score

44. What vendors make products that address the identity federation needs?
<--- Score

45. How are the identity federation's objectives aligned to the group's overall stakeholder strategy?
<--- Score

46. What are the clients issues and concerns?
<--- Score

47. What else needs to be measured?
<--- Score

48. Will it solve real problems?
<--- Score

49. Who needs budgets?
<--- Score

50. Are problem definition and motivation clearly presented?
<--- Score

51. What is the recognized need?
<--- Score

52. What information do users need?
<--- Score

53. Did you miss any major identity federation issues?

<--- Score

54. Do you have/need 24-hour access to key personnel?

<--- Score

55. Are controls defined to recognize and contain problems?

<--- Score

56. Do you need different information or graphics?

<--- Score

57. Where do you need to exercise leadership?

<--- Score

58. What tools and technologies are needed for a custom identity federation project?

<--- Score

59. What identity federation coordination do you need?

<--- Score

60. As a sponsor, customer or management, how important is it to meet goals, objectives?

<--- Score

61. Think about the people you identified for your identity federation project and the project responsibilities you would assign to them, what kind of training do you think they would need to perform these responsibilities effectively?

<--- Score

62. What needs to be done?
<--- Score

63. Which information does the identity federation business case need to include?
<--- Score

64. Will new equipment/products be required to facilitate identity federation delivery, for example is new software needed?
<--- Score

65. Are employees recognized for desired behaviors?
<--- Score

66. Which needs are not included or involved?
<--- Score

67. How are you going to measure success?
<--- Score

68. How do you identify subcontractor relationships?
<--- Score

69. To what extent does each concerned units management team recognize identity federation as an effective investment?
<--- Score

70. Why is this needed?
<--- Score

71. What is the extent or complexity of the identity

federation problem?
<--- Score

72. What needs to stay?
<--- Score

73. How many trainings, in total, are needed?
<--- Score

74. How do you take a forward-looking perspective in identifying identity federation research related to market response and models?
<--- Score

75. What problems are you facing and how do you consider identity federation will circumvent those obstacles?
<--- Score

76. How do you assess your identity federation workforce capability and capacity needs, including skills, competencies, and staffing levels?
<--- Score

77. Is it needed?
<--- Score

78. What resources or support might you need?
<--- Score

79. How do you recognize an identity federation objection?
<--- Score

80. Who needs to know?
<--- Score

81. What is the problem and/or vulnerability?
<--- Score

82. Are there any specific expectations or concerns about the identity federation team, identity federation itself?
<--- Score

83. Are employees recognized or rewarded for performance that demonstrates the highest levels of integrity?
<--- Score

84. Will identity federation deliverables need to be tested and, if so, by whom?
<--- Score

85. What is the identity federation problem definition? What do you need to resolve?
<--- Score

86. Consider your own identity federation project, what types of organizational problems do you think might be causing or affecting your problem, based on the work done so far?
<--- Score

87. Looking at each person individually – does every one have the qualities which are needed to work in this group?
<--- Score

88. How can auditing be a preventative security measure?
<--- Score

89. Who needs what information?
<--- Score

90. Does your organization need more identity federation education?
<--- Score

91. Who else hopes to benefit from it?
<--- Score

92. What identity federation events should you attend?
<--- Score

93. What are the minority interests and what amount of minority interests can be recognized?
<--- Score

94. To what extent would your organization benefit from being recognized as a award recipient?
<--- Score

95. Is it clear when you think of the day ahead of you what activities and tasks you need to complete?
<--- Score

96. Are there regulatory / compliance issues?
<--- Score

97. How much are sponsors, customers, partners, stakeholders involved in identity federation? In other words, what are the risks, if identity federation does not deliver successfully?
<--- Score

Add up total points for this section:
_____ = Total points for this section

Divided by: _____ (number of
statements answered) = _____
Average score for this section

Transfer your score to the identity
federation Index at the beginning of the
Self-Assessment.

CRITERION #2: DEFINE:

INTENT: Formulate the stakeholder problem. Define the problem, needs and objectives.

In my belief, the answer to this question is clearly defined:

5 Strongly Agree

4 Agree

3 Neutral

2 Disagree

1 Strongly Disagree

1. What is a worst-case scenario for losses?
<--- Score

2. Has everyone on the team, including the team leaders, been properly trained?
<--- Score

3. Who defines (or who defined) the rules and roles?

<--- Score

4. Is there regularly 100% attendance at the team meetings? If not, have appointed substitutes attended to preserve cross-functionality and full representation?
<--- Score

5. Do you have a identity federation success story or case study ready to tell and share?
<--- Score

6. What are the core elements of the identity federation business case?
<--- Score

7. What are the record-keeping requirements of identity federation activities?
<--- Score

8. Are the identity federation requirements testable?
<--- Score

9. What identity federation services do you require?
<--- Score

10. How do you keep key subject matter experts in the loop?
<--- Score

11. How do you catch identity federation definition inconsistencies?
<--- Score

12. What identity federation requirements should be

gathered?
<--- Score

13. What specifically is the problem? Where does it occur? When does it occur? What is its extent?
<--- Score

14. Has a identity federation requirement not been met?
<--- Score

15. What critical content must be communicated – who, what, when, where, and how?
<--- Score

16. How often are the team meetings?
<--- Score

17. How have you defined all identity federation requirements first?
<--- Score

18. Does the scope remain the same?
<--- Score

19. Have all of the relationships been defined properly?
<--- Score

20. Is there any additional identity federation definition of success?
<--- Score

21. How do you manage scope?
<--- Score

22. How and when will the baselines be defined?
<--- Score

23. How do you hand over identity federation context?
<--- Score

24. Is the current 'as is' process being followed? If not, what are the discrepancies?
<--- Score

25. What information should you gather?
<--- Score

26. Is scope creep really all bad news?
<--- Score

27. What is out-of-scope initially?
<--- Score

28. Are the identity federation requirements complete?
<--- Score

29. What are the dynamics of the communication plan?
<--- Score

30. How did the identity federation manager receive input to the development of a identity federation improvement plan and the estimated completion dates/times of each activity?
<--- Score

31. Has a team charter been developed and communicated?

<--- Score

32. Are roles and responsibilities formally defined?
<--- Score

33. Do the problem and goal statements meet the SMART criteria (specific, measurable, attainable, relevant, and time-bound)?
<--- Score

34. How do you gather the stories?
<--- Score

35. Where can you gather more information?
<--- Score

36. Have the customer needs been translated into specific, measurable requirements? How?
<--- Score

37. Is the identity federation scope manageable?
<--- Score

38. Have all basic functions of identity federation been defined?
<--- Score

39. Has your scope been defined?
<--- Score

40. What would be the goal or target for a identity federation's improvement team?
<--- Score

41. How do you gather identity federation requirements?

<--- Score

42. Is the improvement team aware of the different versions of a process: what they think it is vs. what it actually is vs. what it should be vs. what it could be?
<--- Score

43. How do you think the partners involved in identity federation would have defined success?
<--- Score

44. What are the rough order estimates on cost savings/opportunities that identity federation brings?
<--- Score

45. Are different versions of process maps needed to account for the different types of inputs?
<--- Score

46. How will variation in the actual durations of each activity be dealt with to ensure that the expected identity federation results are met?
<--- Score

47. Who is gathering information?
<--- Score

48. Are there any constraints known that bear on the ability to perform identity federation work? How is the team addressing them?
<--- Score

49. Who approved the identity federation scope?
<--- Score

50. Is identity federation linked to key stakeholder

goals and objectives?
<--- Score

51. What is the scope?
<--- Score

52. Is data collected and displayed to better understand customer(s) critical needs and requirements.
<--- Score

53. How do you gather requirements?
<--- Score

54. In what way can you redefine the criteria of choice clients have in your category in your favor?
<--- Score

55. Has/have the customer(s) been identified?
<--- Score

56. Does the team have regular meetings?
<--- Score

57. What baselines are required to be defined and managed?
<--- Score

58. Is there a completed, verified, and validated high-level 'as is' (not 'should be' or 'could be') stakeholder process map?
<--- Score

59. What system do you use for gathering identity federation information?
<--- Score

60. Is the team equipped with available and reliable resources?
<--- Score

61. Has a high-level 'as is' process map been completed, verified and validated?
<--- Score

62. Do you all define identity federation in the same way?
<--- Score

63. Will team members regularly document their identity federation work?
<--- Score

64. How will the identity federation team and the group measure complete success of identity federation?
<--- Score

65. How was the 'as is' process map developed, reviewed, verified and validated?
<--- Score

66. What is the scope of identity federation?
<--- Score

67. Are accountability and ownership for identity federation clearly defined?
<--- Score

68. Will a identity federation production readiness review be required?
<--- Score

69. What information do you gather?
<--- Score

70. What is the worst case scenario?
<--- Score

71. How are consistent identity federation definitions important?
<--- Score

72. Have specific policy objectives been defined?
<--- Score

73. How can the value of identity federation be defined?
<--- Score

74. Are task requirements clearly defined?
<--- Score

75. Is there a clear identity federation case definition?
<--- Score

76. When are meeting minutes sent out? Who is on the distribution list?
<--- Score

77. What defines best in class?
<--- Score

78. Has a project plan, Gantt chart, or similar been developed/completed?
<--- Score

79. Has the improvement team collected the 'voice of

the customer' (obtained feedback – qualitative and quantitative)?
<--- Score

80. Will team members perform identity federation work when assigned and in a timely fashion?
<--- Score

81. What customer feedback methods were used to solicit their input?
<--- Score

82. What is out of scope?
<--- Score

83. What was the context?
<--- Score

84. Are customer(s) identified and segmented according to their different needs and requirements?
<--- Score

85. Is the team adequately staffed with the desired cross-functionality? If not, what additional resources are available to the team?
<--- Score

86. What are the Roles and Responsibilities for each team member and its leadership? Where is this documented?
<--- Score

87. Who are the identity federation improvement team members, including Management Leads and Coaches?
<--- Score

88. What is the context?
<--- Score

89. What is the definition of identity federation excellence?
<--- Score

90. What is the scope of the identity federation work?
<--- Score

91. How do you build the right business case?
<--- Score

92. What is the scope of the identity federation effort?
<--- Score

93. What are the identity federation tasks and definitions?
<--- Score

94. Are approval levels defined for contracts and supplements to contracts?
<--- Score

95. What intelligence can you gather?
<--- Score

96. Is there a critical path to deliver identity federation results?
<--- Score

97. How do you manage changes in identity federation requirements?
<--- Score

98. Is identity federation currently on schedule according to the plan?
<--- Score

99. What is the definition of success?
<--- Score

100. Has the direction changed at all during the course of identity federation? If so, when did it change and why?
<--- Score

101. The political context: who holds power?
<--- Score

102. Is it clearly defined in and to your organization what you do?
<--- Score

103. How is the team tracking and documenting its work?
<--- Score

104. Are there different segments of customers?
<--- Score

105. What are the compelling stakeholder reasons for embarking on identity federation?
<--- Score

106. When is the estimated completion date?
<--- Score

107. What scope to assess?
<--- Score

108. Has anyone else (internal or external to the group) attempted to solve this problem or a similar one before? If so, what knowledge can be leveraged from these previous efforts?
<--- Score

109. How do you manage unclear identity federation requirements?
<--- Score

110. How does the identity federation manager ensure against scope creep?
<--- Score

111. How would you define the culture at your organization, how susceptible is it to identity federation changes?
<--- Score

112. What sources do you use to gather information for a identity federation study?
<--- Score

113. What are the tasks and definitions?
<--- Score

114. What happens if identity federation's scope changes?
<--- Score

115. Is the work to date meeting requirements?
<--- Score

116. Is the identity federation scope complete and appropriately sized?
<--- Score

117. How would you define identity federation leadership?
<--- Score

118. What are the boundaries of the scope? What is in bounds and what is not? What is the start point? What is the stop point?
<--- Score

119. If substitutes have been appointed, have they been briefed on the identity federation goals and received regular communications as to the progress to date?
<--- Score

120. Are audit criteria, scope, frequency and methods defined?
<--- Score

121. What constraints exist that might impact the team?
<--- Score

122. What is in scope?
<--- Score

123. Is the scope of identity federation defined?
<--- Score

124. Are resources adequate for the scope?
<--- Score

125. Has the identity federation work been fairly and/or equitably divided and delegated among team members who are qualified and capable to perform

the work? Has everyone contributed?
<--- Score

126. Is there a identity federation management charter, including stakeholder case, problem and goal statements, scope, milestones, roles and responsibilities, communication plan?
<--- Score

127. Is there a completed SIPOC representation, describing the Suppliers, Inputs, Process, Outputs, and Customers?
<--- Score

128. What sort of initial information to gather?
<--- Score

129. When is/was the identity federation start date?
<--- Score

130. What are the identity federation use cases?
<--- Score

131. What are (control) requirements for identity federation Information?
<--- Score

132. Are required metrics defined, what are they?
<--- Score

133. Is identity federation required?
<--- Score

134. What are the requirements for audit information?
<--- Score

135. What knowledge or experience is required?
<--- Score

136. What key stakeholder process output measure(s) does identity federation leverage and how?
<--- Score

137. Why are you doing identity federation and what is the scope?
<--- Score

138. Who is gathering identity federation information?
<--- Score

Add up total points for this section:
_ _ _ _ _ = Total points for this section

Divided by: _ _ _ _ _ _ (number of statements answered) = _ _ _ _ _ _
Average score for this section

Transfer your score to the identity federation Index at the beginning of the Self-Assessment.

CRITERION #3: MEASURE:

INTENT: Gather the correct data.
Measure the current performance and
evolution of the situation.

In my belief, the answer to this
question is clearly defined:

5 Strongly Agree

4 Agree

3 Neutral

2 Disagree

1 Strongly Disagree

1. Who should receive measurement reports?
<--- Score

2. How much does it cost?
<--- Score

**3. What are the costs of delaying identity
federation action?**
<--- Score

4. Are there competing identity federation priorities?
<--- Score

5. What can be used to verify compliance?
<--- Score

6. What is an unallowable cost?
<--- Score

7. How will costs be allocated?
<--- Score

8. How can you measure identity federation in a systematic way?
<--- Score

9. How do you verify your resources?
<--- Score

10. Have you made assumptions about the shape of the future, particularly its impact on your customers and competitors?
<--- Score

11. Is there an opportunity to verify requirements?
<--- Score

12. What details are required of the identity federation cost structure?
<--- Score

13. What are the uncertainties surrounding estimates of impact?
<--- Score

14. Do you effectively measure and reward individual and team performance?
<--- Score

15. How do you control the overall costs of your work processes?
<--- Score

16. What do people want to verify?
<--- Score

17. When should you bother with diagrams?
<--- Score

18. Are there measurements based on task performance?
<--- Score

19. What are the estimated costs of proposed changes?
<--- Score

20. Are identity federation vulnerabilities categorized and prioritized?
<--- Score

21. How can a identity federation test verify your ideas or assumptions?
<--- Score

22. How will measures be used to manage and adapt?
<--- Score

23. Are there any easy-to-implement alternatives to identity federation? Sometimes other solutions are available that do not require the cost implications of a

full-blown project?
<--- Score

24. How do you verify and validate the identity federation data?
<--- Score

25. Do you aggressively reward and promote the people who have the biggest impact on creating excellent identity federation services/products?
<--- Score

26. When are costs are incurred?
<--- Score

27. What are the costs?
<--- Score

28. What would be a real cause for concern?
<--- Score

29. How do you measure variability?
<--- Score

30. What is the total fixed cost?
<--- Score

31. Do the benefits outweigh the costs?
<--- Score

32. What are your key identity federation organizational performance measures, including key short and longer-term financial measures?
<--- Score

33. How will your organization measure success?

<--- Score

34. What tests verify requirements?
<--- Score

35. Has a cost center been established?
<--- Score

36. Where is the cost?
<--- Score

37. What are the current costs of the identity federation process?
<--- Score

38. Are you able to realize any cost savings?
<--- Score

39. What are your customers expectations and measures?
<--- Score

40. Why do you expend time and effort to implement measurement, for whom?
<--- Score

41. What methods are feasible and acceptable to estimate the impact of reforms?
<--- Score

42. Are supply costs steady or fluctuating?
<--- Score

43. What evidence is there and what is measured?
<--- Score

44. What are hidden identity federation quality costs?
<--- Score

45. How do your measurements capture actionable identity federation information for use in exceeding your customers expectations and securing your customers engagement?
<--- Score

46. What is measured? Why?
<--- Score

47. At what cost?
<--- Score

48. What causes mismanagement?
<--- Score

49. What are the types and number of measures to use?
<--- Score

50. How do you aggregate measures across priorities?
<--- Score

51. What are the identity federation investment costs?
<--- Score

52. What measurements are possible, practicable and meaningful?
<--- Score

53. How do you measure success?
<--- Score

54. Are you aware of what could cause a problem?
<--- Score

55. How do you measure efficient delivery of identity federation services?
<--- Score

56. What disadvantage does this cause for the user?
<--- Score

57. What are your operating costs?
<--- Score

58. What happens if cost savings do not materialize?
<--- Score

59. What could cause you to change course?
<--- Score

60. Which identity federation impacts are significant?
<--- Score

61. What does losing customers cost your organization?
<--- Score

62. When a disaster occurs, who gets priority?
<--- Score

63. What is the root cause(s) of the problem?
<--- Score

64. Do you have any cost identity federation limitation requirements?
<--- Score

65. Who pays the cost?

<--- Score

66. Are missed identity federation opportunities costing your organization money?

<--- Score

67. How do you verify the authenticity of the data and information used?

<--- Score

68. What causes investor action?

<--- Score

69. How sensitive must the identity federation strategy be to cost?

<--- Score

70. How can you reduce the costs of obtaining inputs?

<--- Score

71. Which costs should be taken into account?

<--- Score

72. Was a business case (cost/benefit) developed?

<--- Score

73. What measurements are being captured?

<--- Score

74. How do you verify if identity federation is built right?

<--- Score

75. What do you measure and why?

<--- Score

76. Are the units of measure consistent?
<--- Score

77. What does your operating model cost?
<--- Score

78. What are the operational costs after identity federation deployment?
<--- Score

79. Why do the measurements/indicators matter?
<--- Score

80. What potential environmental factors impact the identity federation effort?
<--- Score

81. What does a Test Case verify?
<--- Score

82. Have design-to-cost goals been established?
<--- Score

83. Where is it measured?
<--- Score

84. Are you taking your company in the direction of better and revenue or cheaper and cost?
<--- Score

85. How can you manage cost down?
<--- Score

86. Does the identity federation task fit the client's

priorities?
<--- Score

87. What are the costs of reform?
<--- Score

88. How do you verify performance?
<--- Score

89. How do you measure lifecycle phases?
<--- Score

90. How to cause the change?
<--- Score

91. How long to keep data and how to manage retention costs?
<--- Score

92. What is your identity federation quality cost segregation study?
<--- Score

93. What relevant entities could be measured?
<--- Score

94. What are the strategic priorities for this year?
<--- Score

95. Have you included everything in your identity federation cost models?
<--- Score

96. What harm might be caused?
<--- Score

97. Which measures and indicators matter?

<--- Score

98. How is the value delivered by identity federation being measured?

<--- Score

99. What would it cost to replace your technology?

<--- Score

100. What is the cost of rework?

<--- Score

101. Does management have the right priorities among projects?

<--- Score

102. How do you verify the identity federation requirements quality?

<--- Score

103. Are actual costs in line with budgeted costs?

<--- Score

104. Does a identity federation quantification method exist?

<--- Score

105. What is your decision requirements diagram?

<--- Score

106. Do you have a flow diagram of what happens?

<--- Score

107. How will success or failure be measured?

<--- Score

108. How are measurements made?
<--- Score

109. Did you tackle the cause or the symptom?
<--- Score

110. Will identity federation have an impact on current business continuity, disaster recovery processes and/or infrastructure?
<--- Score

111. What is the total cost related to deploying identity federation, including any consulting or professional services?
<--- Score

112. Is it possible to estimate the impact of unanticipated complexity such as wrong or failed assumptions, feedback, etcetera on proposed reforms?
<--- Score

113. How do you prevent mis-estimating cost?
<--- Score

114. Among the identity federation product and service cost to be estimated, which is considered hardest to estimate?
<--- Score

115. What could cause delays in the schedule?
<--- Score

116. Are the measurements objective?
<--- Score

117. Is the cost worth the identity federation effort ?
<--- Score

118. Do you have an issue in getting priority?
<--- Score

119. How can you measure the performance?
<--- Score

120. What are allowable costs?
<--- Score

121. What is the identity federation business impact?
<--- Score

122. How is progress measured?
<--- Score

123. What are your primary costs, revenues, assets?
<--- Score

124. How do you verify and develop ideas and innovations?
<--- Score

125. Are indirect costs charged to the identity federation program?
<--- Score

126. How will you measure success?
<--- Score

127. What drives O&M cost?
<--- Score

128. How are costs allocated?
<--- Score

129. How do you quantify and qualify impacts?
<--- Score

130. How will you measure your identity federation effectiveness?
<--- Score

131. What are you verifying?
<--- Score

132. How frequently do you track identity federation measures?
<--- Score

133. How will effects be measured?
<--- Score

Add up total points for this section:
_ _ _ _ _ = Total points for this section

Divided by: _ _ _ _ _ _ (number of statements answered) = _ _ _ _ _ _
Average score for this section

Transfer your score to the identity federation Index at the beginning of the Self-Assessment.

CRITERION #4: ANALYZE:

1. How do you measure the operational performance of your key work systems and processes, including productivity, cycle time, and other appropriate measures of process effectiveness, efficiency, and innovation?
<--- Score

2. What qualifications are needed?
<--- Score

3. What internal processes need improvement?
<--- Score

4. Is the performance gap determined?
<--- Score

5. Who owns what data?
<--- Score

6. Have the problem and goal statements been updated to reflect the additional knowledge gained from the analyze phase?
<--- Score

7. What is the oversight process?
<--- Score

8. Was a detailed process map created to amplify critical steps of the 'as is' stakeholder process?
<--- Score

9. What methods do you use to gather identity federation data?
<--- Score

10. Do you understand your management processes today?
<--- Score

11. Are identity federation changes recognized early enough to be approved through the regular process?
<--- Score

12. How much data can be collected in the given timeframe?
<--- Score

13. Do staff qualifications match your project?
<--- Score

14. Is there an established change management process?
<--- Score

15. How often will data be collected for measures?
<--- Score

16. Where is identity federation data gathered?
<--- Score

17. Are you missing identity federation opportunities?
<--- Score

18. What identity federation data will be collected?
<--- Score

19. What identity federation metrics are outputs of the process?
<--- Score

20. Were Pareto charts (or similar) used to portray the 'heavy hitters' (or key sources of variation)?
<--- Score

21. What are the identity federation design outputs?
<--- Score

22. What is the Value Stream Mapping?
<--- Score

23. Have any additional benefits been identified that will result from closing all or most of the gaps?

<--- Score

24. What identity federation data do you gather or use now?
<--- Score

25. What are the necessary qualifications?
<--- Score

26. Is pre-qualification of suppliers carried out?
<--- Score

27. Are your outputs consistent?
<--- Score

28. Is the gap/opportunity displayed and communicated in financial terms?
<--- Score

29. What is your organizations process which leads to recognition of value generation?
<--- Score

30. Who will gather what data?
<--- Score

31. How does the organization define, manage, and improve its identity federation processes?
<--- Score

32. How was the detailed process map generated, verified, and validated?
<--- Score

33. How is the identity federation Value Stream Mapping managed?

<--- Score

34. How do you implement and manage your work processes to ensure that they meet design requirements?
<--- Score

35. Think about some of the processes you undertake within your organization, which do you own?
<--- Score

36. What were the financial benefits resulting from any 'ground fruit or low-hanging fruit' (quick fixes)?
<--- Score

37. What resources go in to get the desired output?
<--- Score

38. Which identity federation data should be retained?
<--- Score

39. Who is involved with workflow mapping?
<--- Score

40. What is your organizations system for selecting qualified vendors?
<--- Score

41. How do you identify specific identity federation investment opportunities and emerging trends?
<--- Score

42. What are the best opportunities for value improvement?
<--- Score

43. How is data used for program management and improvement?

<--- Score

44. What tools were used to narrow the list of possible causes?

<--- Score

45. How do you promote understanding that opportunity for improvement is not criticism of the status quo, or the people who created the status quo?

<--- Score

46. What quality tools were used to get through the analyze phase?

<--- Score

47. How will the identity federation data be captured?

<--- Score

48. Were any designed experiments used to generate additional insight into the data analysis?

<--- Score

49. How has the identity federation data been gathered?

<--- Score

50. Who will facilitate the team and process?

<--- Score

51. What is the identity federation Driver?

<--- Score

52. Do your employees have the opportunity to do

what they do best everyday?
<--- Score

53. What are your outputs?
<--- Score

54. What qualifies as competition?
<--- Score

55. Were there any improvement opportunities identified from the process analysis?
<--- Score

56. Did any value-added analysis or 'lean thinking' take place to identify some of the gaps shown on the 'as is' process map?
<--- Score

57. Can you add value to the current identity federation decision-making process (largely qualitative) by incorporating uncertainty modeling (more quantitative)?
<--- Score

58. Was a cause-and-effect diagram used to explore the different types of causes (or sources of variation)?
<--- Score

59. What are the processes for audit reporting and management?
<--- Score

60. What does the data say about the performance of the stakeholder process?
<--- Score

61. What data do you need to collect?
<--- Score

62. How is the way you as the leader think and process information affecting your organizational culture?
<--- Score

63. How is identity federation data gathered?
<--- Score

64. Do your contracts/agreements contain data security obligations?
<--- Score

65. How do you ensure that the identity federation opportunity is realistic?
<--- Score

66. An organizationally feasible system request is one that considers the mission, goals and objectives of the organization, key questions are: is the identity federation solution request practical and will it solve a problem or take advantage of an opportunity to achieve company goals?
<--- Score

67. Is the final output clearly identified?
<--- Score

68. What are the revised rough estimates of the financial savings/opportunity for identity federation improvements?
<--- Score

69. A compounding model resolution with available relevant data can often provide insight towards a

solution methodology; which identity federation models, tools and techniques are necessary?
<--- Score

70. What successful thing are you doing today that may be blinding you to new growth opportunities?
<--- Score

71. What do you need to qualify?
<--- Score

72. Has an output goal been set?
<--- Score

73. How is the data gathered?
<--- Score

74. What are the identity federation business drivers?
<--- Score

75. What are your key performance measures or indicators and in-process measures for the control and improvement of your identity federation processes?
<--- Score

76. What training and qualifications will you need?
<--- Score

77. What output to create?
<--- Score

78. Where is the data coming from to measure compliance?
<--- Score

79. Who qualifies to gain access to data?
<--- Score

80. What, related to, identity federation processes does your organization outsource?
<--- Score

81. How will the data be checked for quality?
<--- Score

82. How do mission and objectives affect the identity federation processes of your organization?
<--- Score

83. What controls do you have in place to protect data?
<--- Score

84. Is there any way to speed up the process?
<--- Score

85. Do you, as a leader, bounce back quickly from setbacks?
<--- Score

86. What other jobs or tasks affect the performance of the steps in the identity federation process?
<--- Score

87. What is the complexity of the output produced?
<--- Score

88. How difficult is it to qualify what identity federation ROI is?

<--- Score

89. Is the identity federation process severely broken such that a re-design is necessary?
<--- Score

90. What qualifications are necessary?
<--- Score

91. When should a process be art not science?
<--- Score

92. Is the required identity federation data gathered?
<--- Score

93. What conclusions were drawn from the team's data collection and analysis? How did the team reach these conclusions?
<--- Score

94. Are all staff in core identity federation subjects Highly Qualified?
<--- Score

95. What qualifications and skills do you need?
<--- Score

96. How are outputs preserved and protected?
<--- Score

97. What data is gathered?
<--- Score

98. How do your work systems and key work processes relate to and capitalize on your core

competencies?
<--- Score

99. Is there a strict change management process?
<--- Score

100. What are your best practices for minimizing identity federation project risk, while demonstrating incremental value and quick wins throughout the identity federation project lifecycle?
<--- Score

101. What process improvements will be needed?
<--- Score

102. Is the suppliers process defined and controlled?
<--- Score

103. Have you defined which data is gathered how?
<--- Score

104. Who is involved in the management review process?
<--- Score

105. Are all team members qualified for all tasks?
<--- Score

106. What is the cost of poor quality as supported by the team's analysis?
<--- Score

107. What tools were used to generate the list of possible causes?
<--- Score

108. Do quality systems drive continuous improvement?

<--- Score

109. How can risk management be tied procedurally to process elements?

<--- Score

110. Where can you get qualified talent today?

<--- Score

111. Has data output been validated?

<--- Score

112. What are your identity federation processes?

<--- Score

113. What are the personnel training and qualifications required?

<--- Score

114. What did the team gain from developing a sub-process map?

<--- Score

115. Who gets your output?

<--- Score

116. Do several people in different organizational units assist with the identity federation process?

<--- Score

117. What process should you select for improvement?

<--- Score

118. What are the disruptive identity federation technologies that enable your organization to radically change your business processes?
<--- Score

119. What will drive identity federation change?
<--- Score

120. Should you invest in industry-recognized qualifications?
<--- Score

121. Did any additional data need to be collected?
<--- Score

122. Are gaps between current performance and the goal performance identified?
<--- Score

123. What are your current levels and trends in key identity federation measures or indicators of product and process performance that are important to and directly serve your customers?
<--- Score

124. How do you use identity federation data and information to support organizational decision making and innovation?
<--- Score

125. What were the crucial 'moments of truth' on the process map?
<--- Score

126. Do your leaders quickly bounce back from setbacks?

<--- Score

127. Is data and process analysis, root cause analysis and quantifying the gap/opportunity in place?
<--- Score

128. Do you have the authority to produce the output?
<--- Score

129. How do you define collaboration and team output?
<--- Score

130. What qualifications do identity federation leaders need?
<--- Score

131. How will the change process be managed?
<--- Score

132. What identity federation data should be collected?
<--- Score

Add up total points for this section:
_____ = Total points for this section

Divided by: _____ (number of statements answered) = _____
Average score for this section

Transfer your score to the identity federation Index at the beginning of the Self-Assessment.

CRITERION #5: IMPROVE:

INTENT: Develop a practical solution. Innovate, establish and test the solution and to measure the results.

In my belief, the answer to this question is clearly defined:

5 Strongly Agree

4 Agree

3 Neutral

2 Disagree

1 Strongly Disagree

1. How are identity federation risks managed?
<--- Score

2. Who will be using the results of the measurement activities?
<--- Score

3. How do you decide how much to remunerate an employee?

<--- Score

4. What are the affordable identity federation risks?
<--- Score

5. How can you improve performance?
<--- Score

6. Is identity federation documentation maintained?
<--- Score

7. Does a good decision guarantee a good outcome?
<--- Score

8. Who are the identity federation decision makers?
<--- Score

9. Can you integrate quality management and risk management?
<--- Score

10. Was a pilot designed for the proposed solution(s)?
<--- Score

11. How will you know that you have improved?
<--- Score

12. Who manages identity federation risk?
<--- Score

13. What attendant changes will need to be made to ensure that the solution is successful?
<--- Score

14. Do those selected for the identity federation team have a good general understanding of what identity

federation is all about?

<--- Score

15. What tools were most useful during the improve phase?

<--- Score

16. Would you develop a identity federation Communication Strategy?

<--- Score

17. What error proofing will be done to address some of the discrepancies observed in the 'as is' process?

<--- Score

18. What alternative responses are available to manage risk?

<--- Score

19. What is identity federation's impact on utilizing the best solution(s)?

<--- Score

20. Is any identity federation documentation required?

<--- Score

21. What are the implications of the one critical identity federation decision 10 minutes, 10 months, and 10 years from now?

<--- Score

22. What improvements have been achieved?

<--- Score

23. Is the identity federation documentation

thorough?
<--- Score

24. Do vendor agreements bring new compliance risk
?
<--- Score

25. Who controls the risk?
<--- Score

26. How do you keep improving identity federation?
<--- Score

27. How do you measure risk?
<--- Score

28. Can the solution be designed and implemented within an acceptable time period?
<--- Score

29. Is there any other identity federation solution?
<--- Score

30. What to do with the results or outcomes of measurements?
<--- Score

31. What tools do you use once you have decided on a identity federation strategy and more importantly how do you choose?
<--- Score

32. Where do the identity federation decisions reside?
<--- Score

33. identity federation risk decisions: whose call Is It?

<--- Score

34. What went well, what should change, what can improve?
<--- Score

35. How does your organization evaluate strategic identity federation success?
<--- Score

36. Who do you report identity federation results to?
<--- Score

37. Are the key business and technology risks being managed?
<--- Score

38. Are the most efficient solutions problem-specific?
<--- Score

39. Can you identify any significant risks or exposures to identity federation third- parties (vendors, service providers, alliance partners etc) that concern you?
<--- Score

40. How can you improve identity federation?
<--- Score

41. How will you measure the results?
<--- Score

42. Are risk triggers captured?
<--- Score

43. Which identity federation solution is appropriate?
<--- Score

44. How is continuous improvement applied to risk management?
<--- Score

45. Is the identity federation risk managed?
<--- Score

46. How risky is your organization?
<--- Score

47. How do you improve productivity?
<--- Score

48. How is knowledge sharing about risk management improved?
<--- Score

49. Are procedures documented for managing identity federation risks?
<--- Score

50. Who are the identity federation decision-makers?
<--- Score

51. Why improve in the first place?
<--- Score

52. Are the risks fully understood, reasonable and manageable?
<--- Score

53. What is the identity federation's sustainability risk?
<--- Score

54. Was a identity federation charter developed?

<--- Score

55. Who makes the identity federation decisions in your organization?
<--- Score

56. What assumptions are made about the solution and approach?
<--- Score

57. How do you improve identity federation service perception, and satisfaction?
<--- Score

58. What is the risk?
<--- Score

59. How risky is your organization?
<--- Score

60. What lessons, if any, from a pilot were incorporated into the design of the full-scale solution?
<--- Score

61. Is the measure of success for identity federation understandable to a variety of people?
<--- Score

62. What criteria will you use to assess your identity federation risks?
<--- Score

63. How are policy decisions made and where?
<--- Score

64. Are risk management tasks balanced centrally and

locally?
<--- Score

65. How do you link measurement and risk?
<--- Score

66. What are the concrete identity federation results?
<--- Score

67. Are events managed to resolution?
<--- Score

68. What tools were used to tap into the creativity and encourage 'outside the box' thinking?
<--- Score

69. Is supporting identity federation documentation required?
<--- Score

70. How do you measure improved identity federation service perception, and satisfaction?
<--- Score

71. How do you go about comparing identity federation approaches/solutions?
<--- Score

72. Who are the people involved in developing and implementing identity federation?
<--- Score

73. What strategies for identity federation improvement are successful?
<--- Score

74. What is the magnitude of the improvements?
<--- Score

75. Is there a high likelihood that any recommendations will achieve their intended results?
<--- Score

76. How do you manage and improve your identity federation work systems to deliver customer value and achieve organizational success and sustainability?
<--- Score

77. Are you assessing identity federation and risk?
<--- Score

78. Is the solution technically practical?
<--- Score

79. What were the criteria for evaluating a identity federation pilot?
<--- Score

80. How can the phases of identity federation development be identified?
<--- Score

81. When you map the key players in your own work and the types/domains of relationships with them, which relationships do you find easy and which challenging, and why?
<--- Score

82. Is the scope clearly documented?
<--- Score

83. How do the identity federation results compare

with the performance of your competitors and other organizations with similar offerings?
<--- Score

84. Do you combine technical expertise with business knowledge and identity federation Key topics include lifecycles, development approaches, requirements and how to make a business case?
<--- Score

85. How do you deal with identity federation risk?
<--- Score

86. What does the 'should be' process map/design look like?
<--- Score

87. Is the identity federation solution sustainable?
<--- Score

88. Were any criteria developed to assist the team in testing and evaluating potential solutions?
<--- Score

89. What are your current levels and trends in key measures or indicators of workforce and leader development?
<--- Score

90. Is risk periodically assessed?
<--- Score

91. How do you mitigate identity federation risk?
<--- Score

92. Have you achieved identity federation

improvements?
<--- Score

93. What identity federation improvements can be made?
<--- Score

94. What communications are necessary to support the implementation of the solution?
<--- Score

95. Explorations of the frontiers of identity federation will help you build influence, improve identity federation, optimize decision making, and sustain change, what is your approach?
<--- Score

96. What is the team's contingency plan for potential problems occurring in implementation?
<--- Score

97. Risk factors: what are the characteristics of identity federation that make it risky?
<--- Score

98. What are the expected identity federation results?
<--- Score

99. What current systems have to be understood and/or changed?
<--- Score

100. Who should make the identity federation decisions?
<--- Score

101. What risks do you need to manage?

<--- Score

102. What area needs the greatest improvement?

<--- Score

103. Have you identified breakpoints and/or risk tolerances that will trigger broad consideration of a potential need for intervention or modification of strategy?

<--- Score

104. Who manages supplier risk management in your organization?

<--- Score

105. What can you do to improve?

<--- Score

106. In the past few months, what is the smallest change you have made that has had the biggest positive result? What was it about that small change that produced the large return?

<--- Score

107. Who will be responsible for documenting the identity federation requirements in detail?

<--- Score

108. For estimation problems, how do you develop an estimation statement?

<--- Score

109. For decision problems, how do you develop a decision statement?

<--- Score

110. Does the goal represent a desired result that can be measured?

<--- Score

111. How can you better manage risk?

<--- Score

112. What do you want to improve?

<--- Score

113. Will the controls trigger any other risks?

<--- Score

114. Who will be responsible for making the decisions to include or exclude requested changes once identity federation is underway?

<--- Score

115. What needs improvement? Why?

<--- Score

116. What were the underlying assumptions on the cost-benefit analysis?

<--- Score

117. What tools were used to evaluate the potential solutions?

<--- Score

118. Which of the recognised risks out of all risks can be most likely transferred?

<--- Score

119. How can skill-level changes improve identity federation?

<--- Score

120. How significant is the improvement in the eyes of the end user?
<--- Score

121. Do you cover the five essential competencies: Communication, Collaboration,Innovation, Adaptability, and Leadership that improve an organizations ability to leverage the new identity federation in a volatile global economy?
<--- Score

122. What actually has to improve and by how much?
<--- Score

123. Who are the key stakeholders for the identity federation evaluation?
<--- Score

124. How do you define the solutions' scope?
<--- Score

125. What is identity federation risk?
<--- Score

126. How scalable is your identity federation solution?
<--- Score

127. Do you need to do a usability evaluation?
<--- Score

128. Are decisions made in a timely manner?
<--- Score

129. How does the team improve its work?
<--- Score

130. To what extent does management recognize identity federation as a tool to increase the results?
<--- Score

131. How will you know that a change is an improvement?
<--- Score

132. Who controls key decisions that will be made?
<--- Score

133. What practices helps your organization to develop its capacity to recognize patterns?
<--- Score

134. Risk events: what are the things that could go wrong?
<--- Score

135. How will you recognize and celebrate results?
<--- Score

136. If you could go back in time five years, what decision would you make differently? What is your best guess as to what decision you're making today you might regret five years from now?
<--- Score

137. What is the implementation plan?
<--- Score

138. How do you manage identity federation risk?
<--- Score

139. Risk Identification: What are the possible risk events your organization faces in relation to identity federation?
<--- Score

140. How will you know when its improved?
<--- Score

    Add up total points for this section:
    _ _ _ _ _ = Total points for this section

    Divided by: _ _ _ _ _ _ (number of statements answered) = _ _ _ _ _ _
    Average score for this section

    Transfer your score to the identity federation Index at the beginning of the Self-Assessment.

CRITERION #6: CONTROL:

INTENT: Implement the practical solution. Maintain the performance and correct possible complications.

In my belief, the answer to this question is clearly defined:

5 Strongly Agree

4 Agree

3 Neutral

2 Disagree

1 Strongly Disagree

1. Is there a control plan in place for sustaining improvements (short and long-term)?
<--- Score

2. Who is the identity federation process owner?
<--- Score

3. Are new process steps, standards, and documentation ingrained into normal operations?

<--- Score

4. How will new or emerging customer needs/requirements be checked/communicated to orient the process toward meeting the new specifications and continually reducing variation?
<--- Score

5. What are the critical parameters to watch?
<--- Score

6. Has the improved process and its steps been standardized?
<--- Score

7. Is the identity federation test/monitoring cost justified?
<--- Score

8. How do you encourage people to take control and responsibility?
<--- Score

9. How will the process owner verify improvement in present and future sigma levels, process capabilities?
<--- Score

10. Are suggested corrective/restorative actions indicated on the response plan for known causes to problems that might surface?
<--- Score

11. Are documented procedures clear and easy to follow for the operators?
<--- Score

12. What other systems, operations, processes, and infrastructures (hiring practices, staffing, training, incentives/rewards, metrics/dashboards/scorecards, etc.) need updates, additions, changes, or deletions in order to facilitate knowledge transfer and improvements?
<--- Score

13. What are the performance and scale of the identity federation tools?
<--- Score

14. Where do ideas that reach policy makers and planners as proposals for identity federation strengthening and reform actually originate?
<--- Score

15. Who controls critical resources?
<--- Score

16. Are the planned controls in place?
<--- Score

17. Is there a documented and implemented monitoring plan?
<--- Score

18. Is new knowledge gained imbedded in the response plan?
<--- Score

19. How will you measure your QA plan's effectiveness?
<--- Score

20. How do you plan on providing proper recognition

and disclosure of supporting companies?
<--- Score

21. What identity federation standards are applicable?
<--- Score

22. Is there a transfer of ownership and knowledge to process owner and process team tasked with the responsibilities.
<--- Score

23. How is identity federation project cost planned, managed, monitored?
<--- Score

24. How do you plan for the cost of succession?
<--- Score

25. How do senior leaders actions reflect a commitment to the organizations identity federation values?
<--- Score

26. You may have created your quality measures at a time when you lacked resources, technology wasn't up to the required standard, or low service levels were the industry norm. Have those circumstances changed?
<--- Score

27. What is the control/monitoring plan?
<--- Score

28. How do your controls stack up?
<--- Score

29. How do you establish and deploy modified action plans if circumstances require a shift in plans and rapid execution of new plans?
<--- Score

30. Who sets the identity federation standards?
<--- Score

31. How will identity federation decisions be made and monitored?
<--- Score

32. Do you monitor the identity federation decisions made and fine tune them as they evolve?
<--- Score

33. Do the viable solutions scale to future needs?
<--- Score

34. Are you measuring, monitoring and predicting identity federation activities to optimize operations and profitability, and enhancing outcomes?
<--- Score

35. Does job training on the documented procedures need to be part of the process team's education and training?
<--- Score

36. In the case of a identity federation project, the criteria for the audit derive from implementation objectives, an audit of a identity federation project involves assessing whether the recommendations outlined for implementation have been met, can you track that any identity federation project is

implemented as planned, and is it working?
<--- Score

37. How will the day-to-day responsibilities for monitoring and continual improvement be transferred from the improvement team to the process owner?
<--- Score

38. How is change control managed?
<--- Score

39. Is there a recommended audit plan for routine surveillance inspections of identity federation's gains?
<--- Score

40. How do controls support value?
<--- Score

41. Are pertinent alerts monitored, analyzed and distributed to appropriate personnel?
<--- Score

42. What is the best design framework for identity federation organization now that, in a post industrial-age if the top-down, command and control model is no longer relevant?
<--- Score

43. What do your reports reflect?
<--- Score

44. What do you measure to verify effectiveness gains?
<--- Score

45. How might the group capture best practices and lessons learned so as to leverage improvements?
<--- Score

46. How likely is the current identity federation plan to come in on schedule or on budget?
<--- Score

47. Are operating procedures consistent?
<--- Score

48. How will input, process, and output variables be checked to detect for sub-optimal conditions?
<--- Score

49. How do you monitor usage and cost?
<--- Score

50. Is there a standardized process?
<--- Score

51. What is the standard for acceptable identity federation performance?
<--- Score

52. What should the next improvement project be that is related to identity federation?
<--- Score

53. What quality tools were useful in the control phase?
<--- Score

54. How will the process owner and team be able to hold the gains?
<--- Score

55. Will any special training be provided for results interpretation?
<--- Score

56. Does the response plan contain a definite closed loop continual improvement scheme (e.g., plan-do-check-act)?
<--- Score

57. Implementation Planning: is a pilot needed to test the changes before a full roll out occurs?
<--- Score

58. Has the identity federation value of standards been quantified?
<--- Score

59. Will your goals reflect your program budget?
<--- Score

60. How can you best use all of your knowledge repositories to enhance learning and sharing?
<--- Score

61. Have new or revised work instructions resulted?
<--- Score

62. What are your results for key measures or indicators of the accomplishment of your identity federation strategy and action plans, including building and strengthening core competencies?
<--- Score

63. What are the known security controls?
<--- Score

64. What other areas of the group might benefit from the identity federation team's improvements, knowledge, and learning?
<--- Score

65. How will report readings be checked to effectively monitor performance?
<--- Score

66. What are the key elements of your identity federation performance improvement system, including your evaluation, organizational learning, and innovation processes?
<--- Score

67. How do you spread information?
<--- Score

68. What adjustments to the strategies are needed?
<--- Score

69. Is there a identity federation Communication plan covering who needs to get what information when?
<--- Score

70. Is knowledge gained on process shared and institutionalized?
<--- Score

71. What key inputs and outputs are being measured on an ongoing basis?
<--- Score

72. Does the identity federation performance meet the customer's requirements?

<--- Score

73. What are customers monitoring?
<--- Score

74. Who has control over resources?
<--- Score

75. What can you control?
<--- Score

76. How widespread is its use?
<--- Score

77. Is there documentation that will support the successful operation of the improvement?
<--- Score

78. Against what alternative is success being measured?
<--- Score

79. Do you monitor the effectiveness of your identity federation activities?
<--- Score

80. Act/Adjust: What Do you Need to Do Differently?
<--- Score

81. Will the team be available to assist members in planning investigations?
<--- Score

82. Can support from partners be adjusted?
<--- Score

83. Can you adapt and adjust to changing identity federation situations?
<--- Score

84. Who will be in control?
<--- Score

85. What do you stand for--and what are you against?
<--- Score

86. What are you attempting to measure/monitor?
<--- Score

87. Who is going to spread your message?
<--- Score

88. What is your plan to assess your security risks?
<--- Score

89. How do you select, collect, align, and integrate identity federation data and information for tracking daily operations and overall organizational performance, including progress relative to strategic objectives and action plans?
<--- Score

90. Are controls in place and consistently applied?
<--- Score

91. Is reporting being used or needed?
<--- Score

92. Are the identity federation standards challenging?
<--- Score

93. Is a response plan in place for when the input,

process, or output measures indicate an 'out-of-control' condition?
<--- Score

94. Does a troubleshooting guide exist or is it needed?
<--- Score

95. Are there documented procedures?
<--- Score

96. Does identity federation appropriately measure and monitor risk?
<--- Score

97. Is a response plan established and deployed?
<--- Score

98. What is the recommended frequency of auditing?
<--- Score

Add up total points for this section:
_ _ _ _ _ = Total points for this section

Divided by: _ _ _ _ _ _ (number of statements answered) = _ _ _ _ _ _
Average score for this section

Transfer your score to the identity federation Index at the beginning of the Self-Assessment.

CRITERION #7: SUSTAIN:

INTENT: Retain the benefits.

In my belief, the answer to this question is clearly defined:

5 Strongly Agree

4 Agree

3 Neutral

2 Disagree

1 Strongly Disagree

1. How do you determine the key elements that affect identity federation workforce satisfaction, how are these elements determined for different workforce groups and segments?
<--- Score

2. How will you ensure you get what you expected?
<--- Score

3. To whom do you add value?
<--- Score

4. How will you insure seamless interoperability of identity federation moving forward?
<--- Score

5. How do you listen to customers to obtain actionable information?
<--- Score

6. What happens when a new employee joins the organization?
<--- Score

7. What are you trying to prove to yourself, and how might it be hijacking your life and business success?
<--- Score

8. Are you maintaining a past–present–future perspective throughout the identity federation discussion?
<--- Score

9. What identity federation skills are most important?
<--- Score

10. What was the last experiment you ran?
<--- Score

11. Who are the key stakeholders?
<--- Score

12. How do you accomplish your long range identity federation goals?
<--- Score

13. At what moment would you think; Will I get fired?

<--- Score

14. What trophy do you want on your mantle?
<--- Score

15. What are your personal philosophies regarding identity federation and how do they influence your work?
<--- Score

16. What unique value proposition (UVP) do you offer?
<--- Score

17. Who do you think the world wants your organization to be?
<--- Score

18. Are the criteria for selecting recommendations stated?
<--- Score

19. Why will customers want to buy your organizations products/services?
<--- Score

20. If you find that you havent accomplished one of the goals for one of the steps of the identity federation strategy, what will you do to fix it?
<--- Score

21. Operational - will it work?
<--- Score

22. Is it economical; do you have the time and money?

<--- Score

23. How do you proactively clarify deliverables and identity federation quality expectations?
<--- Score

24. How do you provide a safe environment -physically and emotionally?
<--- Score

25. What must you excel at?
<--- Score

26. How do customers see your organization?
<--- Score

27. What may be the consequences for the performance of an organization if all stakeholders are not consulted regarding identity federation?
<--- Score

28. How are you doing compared to your industry?
<--- Score

29. Which functions and people interact with the supplier and or customer?
<--- Score

30. Why is identity federation important for you now?
<--- Score

31. In retrospect, of the projects that you pulled the plug on, what percent do you wish had been allowed to keep going, and what percent do you wish had ended earlier?

<--- Score

32. What could happen if you do not do it?
<--- Score

33. Do you think you know, or do you know you know
?
<--- Score

34. What management system can you use to leverage the identity federation experience, ideas, and concerns of the people closest to the work to be done?
<--- Score

35. What happens at your organization when people fail?
<--- Score

36. What identity federation modifications can you make work for you?
<--- Score

37. What are the top 3 things at the forefront of your identity federation agendas for the next 3 years?
<--- Score

38. Who are your customers?
<--- Score

39. How do you manage identity federation Knowledge Management (KM)?
<--- Score

40. What would have to be true for the option on the table to be the best possible choice?

<--- Score

41. Is your strategy driving your strategy? Or is the way in which you allocate resources driving your strategy?
<--- Score

42. What have you done to protect your business from competitive encroachment?
<--- Score

43. Will it be accepted by users?
<--- Score

44. Who will determine interim and final deadlines?
<--- Score

45. What are specific identity federation rules to follow?
<--- Score

46. What knowledge, skills and characteristics mark a good identity federation project manager?
<--- Score

47. Would you rather sell to knowledgeable and informed customers or to uninformed customers?
<--- Score

48. Who will be responsible for deciding whether identity federation goes ahead or not after the initial investigations?
<--- Score

49. How do senior leaders deploy your organizations

vision and values through your leadership system, to the workforce, to key suppliers and partners, and to customers and other stakeholders, as appropriate?
<--- Score

50. What is the overall talent health of your organization as a whole at senior levels, and for each organization reporting to a member of the Senior Leadership Team?
<--- Score

51. What happens if you do not have enough funding?
<--- Score

52. What is your formula for success in identity federation ?
<--- Score

53. What role does communication play in the success or failure of a identity federation project?
<--- Score

54. What are the long-term identity federation goals?
<--- Score

55. How do you engage the workforce, in addition to satisfying them?
<--- Score

56. If you weren't already in this business, would you enter it today? And if not, what are you going to do about it?
<--- Score

57. Who do we want your customers to become?

<--- Score

58. How do you keep records, of what?
<--- Score

59. Is there a work around that you can use?
<--- Score

60. What stupid rule would you most like to kill?
<--- Score

61. Is maximizing identity federation protection the same as minimizing identity federation loss?
<--- Score

62. Are assumptions made in identity federation stated explicitly?
<--- Score

63. Who else should you help?
<--- Score

64. Is your basic point _____ or _____?
<--- Score

65. If you had to leave your organization for a year and the only communication you could have with employees/colleagues was a single paragraph, what would you write?
<--- Score

66. What did you miss in the interview for the worst hire you ever made?
<--- Score

67. How do you create buy-in?

<--- Score

68. Who do you want your customers to become?
<--- Score

69. How important is identity federation to the user organizations mission?
<--- Score

70. How do you set identity federation stretch targets and how do you get people to not only participate in setting these stretch targets but also that they strive to achieve these?
<--- Score

71. What is your identity federation strategy?
<--- Score

72. What is the overall business strategy?
<--- Score

73. Do you say no to customers for no reason?
<--- Score

74. How do you govern and fulfill your societal responsibilities?
<--- Score

75. What relationships among identity federation trends do you perceive?
<--- Score

76. Who uses your product in ways you never expected?
<--- Score

77. Why do and why don't your customers like your organization?

<--- Score

78. Instead of going to current contacts for new ideas, what if you reconnected with dormant contacts--the people you used to know? If you were going reactivate a dormant tie, who would it be?

<--- Score

79. Whose voice (department, ethnic group, women, older workers, etc) might you have missed hearing from in your company, and how might you amplify this voice to create positive momentum for your business?

<--- Score

80. How do you deal with identity federation changes?

<--- Score

81. What projects are going on in the organization today, and what resources are those projects using from the resource pools?

<--- Score

82. How will you know that the identity federation project has been successful?

<--- Score

83. Who is the main stakeholder, with ultimate responsibility for driving identity federation forward?

<--- Score

84. Who, on the executive team or the board, has spoken to a customer recently?

<--- Score

85. How is implementation research currently incorporated into each of your goals?

<--- Score

86. What trouble can you get into?

<--- Score

87. What are current identity federation paradigms?

<--- Score

88. How can you negotiate identity federation successfully with a stubborn boss, an irate client, or a deceitful coworker?

<--- Score

89. Are the assumptions believable and achievable?

<--- Score

90. What is the funding source for this project?

<--- Score

91. What are strategies for increasing support and reducing opposition?

<--- Score

92. What are the short and long-term identity federation goals?

<--- Score

93. Who is responsible for identity federation?

<--- Score

94. What goals did you miss?
<--- Score

95. What have been your experiences in defining long range identity federation goals?
<--- Score

96. Is a identity federation team work effort in place?
<--- Score

97. Did your employees make progress today?
<--- Score

98. What is the purpose of identity federation in relation to the mission?
<--- Score

99. Who is responsible for errors?
<--- Score

100. How do you lead with identity federation in mind?
<--- Score

101. Marketing budgets are tighter, consumers are more skeptical, and social media has changed forever the way we talk about identity federation, how do you gain traction?
<--- Score

102. Think of your identity federation project, what are the main functions?
<--- Score

103. What does your signature ensure?
<--- Score

104. What business benefits will identity federation goals deliver if achieved?
<--- Score

105. Can you maintain your growth without detracting from the factors that have contributed to your success?
<--- Score

106. What are the gaps in your knowledge and experience?
<--- Score

107. If you do not follow, then how to lead?
<--- Score

108. What will be the consequences to the stakeholder (financial, reputation etc) if identity federation does not go ahead or fails to deliver the objectives?
<--- Score

109. How do you know if you are successful?
<--- Score

110. What is your question? Why?
<--- Score

111. What is the recommended frequency of auditing?
<--- Score

112. Are you changing as fast as the world around you?

<--- Score

113. Is a identity federation breakthrough on the horizon?
<--- Score

114. Which models, tools and techniques are necessary?
<--- Score

115. Do you have an implicit bias for capital investments over people investments?
<--- Score

116. Do you have the right capabilities and capacities?
<--- Score

117. What is the estimated value of the project?
<--- Score

118. How long will it take to change?
<--- Score

119. In the past year, what have you done (or could you have done) to increase the accurate perception of your company/brand as ethical and honest?
<--- Score

120. Do you know who is a friend or a foe?
<--- Score

121. Can you do all this work?
<--- Score

122. What is the source of the strategies for identity federation strengthening and reform?
<--- Score

123. How do you foster the skills, knowledge, talents, attributes, and characteristics you want to have?
<--- Score

124. What is the kind of project structure that would be appropriate for your identity federation project, should it be formal and complex, or can it be less formal and relatively simple?
<--- Score

125. Who is responsible for ensuring appropriate resources (time, people and money) are allocated to identity federation?
<--- Score

126. How do you make it meaningful in connecting identity federation with what users do day-to-day?
<--- Score

127. How do you ensure that implementations of identity federation products are done in a way that ensures safety?
<--- Score

128. What are the rules and assumptions your industry operates under? What if the opposite were true?
<--- Score

129. Who are four people whose careers you have enhanced?
<--- Score

130. Do you know what you are doing? And who do you call if you don't?

<--- Score

131. If you were responsible for initiating and implementing major changes in your organization, what steps might you take to ensure acceptance of those changes?

<--- Score

132. What is a feasible sequencing of reform initiatives over time?

<--- Score

133. Are all key stakeholders present at all Structured Walkthroughs?

<--- Score

134. What are the potential basics of identity federation fraud?

<--- Score

135. How do you go about securing identity federation?

<--- Score

136. Whom among your colleagues do you trust, and for what?

<--- Score

137. How do you maintain identity federation's Integrity?

<--- Score

138. Why is it important to have senior management support for a identity federation

project?
<--- Score

139. What new services of functionality will be implemented next with identity federation ?
<--- Score

140. What is your BATNA (best alternative to a negotiated agreement)?
<--- Score

141. What one word do you want to own in the minds of your customers, employees, and partners?
<--- Score

142. What are the business goals identity federation is aiming to achieve?
<--- Score

143. If you got fired and a new hire took your place, what would she do different?
<--- Score

144. Is there any reason to believe the opposite of my current belief?
<--- Score

145. What information is critical to your organization that your executives are ignoring?
<--- Score

146. What are the essentials of internal identity federation management?
<--- Score

147. What counts that you are not counting?

<--- Score

148. What is something you believe that nearly no one agrees with you on?
<--- Score

149. What are the success criteria that will indicate that identity federation objectives have been met and the benefits delivered?
<--- Score

150. How do you track customer value, profitability or financial return, organizational success, and sustainability?
<--- Score

151. Do you think identity federation accomplishes the goals you expect it to accomplish?
<--- Score

152. Political -is anyone trying to undermine this project?
<--- Score

153. What is your competitive advantage?
<--- Score

154. Who will provide the final approval of identity federation deliverables?
<--- Score

155. Are you paying enough attention to the partners your company depends on to succeed?
<--- Score

156. Are you making progress, and are you making progress as identity federation leaders?
<--- Score

157. What is it like to work for you?
<--- Score

158. When information truly is ubiquitous, when reach and connectivity are completely global, when computing resources are infinite, and when a whole new set of impossibilities are not only possible, but happening, what will that do to your business?
<--- Score

159. Where can you break convention?
<--- Score

160. In a project to restructure identity federation outcomes, which stakeholders would you involve?
<--- Score

161. What are the key enablers to make this identity federation move?
<--- Score

162. What are the barriers to increased identity federation production?
<--- Score

163. Do you have enough freaky customers in your portfolio pushing you to the limit day in and day out?
<--- Score

164. What is the craziest thing you can do?
<--- Score

165. Who is on the team?
<--- Score

166. Why should people listen to you?
<--- Score

167. Which identity federation goals are the most important?
<--- Score

168. Do you feel that more should be done in the identity federation area?
<--- Score

169. How do you transition from the baseline to the target?
<--- Score

170. Can the schedule be done in the given time?
<--- Score

171. Is identity federation realistic, or are you setting yourself up for failure?
<--- Score

172. What should you stop doing?
<--- Score

173. What is effective identity federation?
<--- Score

174. What are you challenging?
<--- Score

175. How will you motivate the stakeholders with the

least vested interest?
<--- Score

176. What would you recommend your friend do if he/she were facing this dilemma?
<--- Score

177. Is the identity federation organization completing tasks effectively and efficiently?
<--- Score

178. What you are going to do to affect the numbers?
<--- Score

179. Ask yourself: how would you do this work if you only had one staff member to do it?
<--- Score

Add up total points for this section:
_ _ _ _ _ = Total points for this section

Divided by: _ _ _ _ _ _ (number of statements answered) = _ _ _ _ _ _
Average score for this section

Transfer your score to the identity federation Index at the beginning of the Self-Assessment.

Identity Federation and Managing Projects, Criteria for Project Managers:

1.0 Initiating Process Group: Identity Federation

1. How well defined and documented were the Identity Federation project management processes you chose to use?

2. What were things that you did well, and could improve, and how?

3. How to control and approve each phase?

4. Does the Identity Federation project team have enough people to execute the Identity Federation project plan?

5. Are there resources to maintain and support the outcome of the Identity Federation project?

6. What must be done?

7. At which stage, in a typical Identity Federation project do stake holders have maximum influence?

8. Were escalated issues resolved promptly?

9. Although the Identity Federation project manager does not directly manage procurement and contracting activities, who does manage procurement and contracting activities in your organization then if not the PM?

10. How will it affect me?

11. What are the short and long term implications?

12. Are the Identity Federation project team and stakeholders meeting regularly and using a meeting agenda and taking notes to accurately document what is being covered and what happened in the weekly meetings?

13. What are the required resources?

14. In which Identity Federation project management process group is the detailed Identity Federation project budget created?

15. What were the challenges that you encountered during the execution of a previous Identity Federation project that you would not want to repeat?

16. How well did the chosen processes produce the expected results?

17. How do you help others satisfy needs?

18. What are the inputs required to produce the deliverables?

19. Do you understand the quality and control criteria that must be achieved for successful Identity Federation project completion?

20. What are the overarching issues of your organization?

1.1 Project Charter: Identity Federation

21. What are you trying to accomplish?

22. Is it an improvement over existing products?

23. Identity Federation project deliverables: what is the Identity Federation project going to produce?

24. Fit with other Products Compliments – Cannibalizes?

25. When?

26. Run it as as a startup?

27. Where and how does the team fit within your organization structure?

28. Why do you manage integration?

29. Are there special technology requirements?

30. Assumptions: what factors, for planning purposes, are you considering to be true?

31. Must Have?

32. How much?

33. Pop quiz – which are the same inputs as in the Identity Federation project charter?

34. Who are the stakeholders?

35. Success determination factors: how will the success of the Identity Federation project be determined from the customers perspective?

36. What is the most common tool for helping define the detail?

37. What changes can you make to improve?

38. Where does all this information come from?

39. What are the assumptions?

40. Why have you chosen the aim you have set forth?

1.2 Stakeholder Register: Identity Federation

41. What is the power of the stakeholder?

42. What & Why?

43. How should employers make voices heard?

44. What are the major Identity Federation project milestones requiring communications or providing communications opportunities?

45. How will reports be created?

46. How much influence do they have on the Identity Federation project?

47. Who is managing stakeholder engagement?

48. Is your organization ready for change?

49. How big is the gap?

50. What opportunities exist to provide communications?

51. Who wants to talk about Security?

1.3 Stakeholder Analysis Matrix: Identity Federation

52. Who will be affected by the work?

53. What is the issue at stake?

54. What tools would help you communicate?

55. Are the interests in line with the program objectives?

56. Advantages of proposition?

57. Could any of your organizations weaknesses seriously threaten development?

58. Organizational Applicability?

59. Insurmountable weaknesses?

60. Who will be responsible for managing the outcome?

61. What do you Evaluate?

62. Vital contracts and partners?

63. Who has not been involved up to now and should have been?

64. Environmental effects?

65. Legislative effects?

66. What obstacles does your organization face?

67. Inoculations or payment to receive them?

68. Competitor intentions - various?

69. What resources might the stakeholder bring to the Identity Federation project?

70. How do they affect the Identity Federation project and its outcomes?

2.0 Planning Process Group: Identity Federation

71. How do you integrate Identity Federation project Planning with the Iterative/Evolutionary SDLC?

72. What is the NEXT thing to do?

73. Are you just doing busywork to pass the time?

74. Is the Identity Federation project supported by national and/or local organizations?

75. Who are the Identity Federation project stakeholders?

76. Identity Federation project assessment; why did you do this Identity Federation project?

77. What input will you be required to provide the Identity Federation project team?

78. To what extent is the program helping to influence your organizations policy framework?

79. What should you do next?

80. Does the program have follow-up mechanisms (to verify the quality of the products, punctuality of delivery, etc.) to measure progress in the achievement of the envisaged results?

81. How well do the team follow the chosen

processes?

82. What is involved in Identity Federation project scope management, and why is good Identity Federation project scope management so important on information technology Identity Federation projects?

83. Is the pace of implementing the products of the program ensuring the completeness of the results of the Identity Federation project?

84. Is the schedule for the set products being met?

85. You are creating your WBS and find that you keep decomposing tasks into smaller and smaller units. How can you tell when you are done?

86. Are the necessary foundations in place to ensure the sustainability of the results of the Identity Federation project?

87. How will you do it?

88. Will you be replaced?

89. Why do it Identity Federation projects fail?

90. On which process should team members spend the most time?

2.1 Project Management Plan: Identity Federation

91. Will you add a schedule and diagram?

92. Why Change?

93. What worked well?

94. Does the selected plan protect privacy?

95. What data/reports/tools/etc. do your PMs need?

96. Is there an incremental analysis/cost effectiveness analysis of proposed mitigation features based on an approved method and using an accepted model?

97. What is the business need?

98. Is mitigation authorized or recommended?

99. Are comparable cost estimates used for comparing, screening and selecting alternative plans, and has a reasonable cost estimate been developed for the recommended plan?

100. Is there anything you would now do differently on your Identity Federation project based on past experience?

101. What would you do differently what did not work?

102. When is the Identity Federation project management plan created?

103. What are the assigned resources?

104. Was the peer (technical) review of the cost estimates duly coordinated with the cost estimate center of expertise and addressed in the review documentation and certification?

105. What goes into your Identity Federation project Charter?

106. If the Identity Federation project management plan is a comprehensive document that guides you in Identity Federation project execution and control, then what should it NOT contain?

107. How well are you able to manage your risk?

108. Is the engineering content at a feasibility level-of-detail, and is it sufficiently complete, to provide an adequate basis for the baseline cost estimate?

109. Are there any scope changes proposed for a previously authorized Identity Federation project?

110. What is Identity Federation project scope management?

2.2 Scope Management Plan: Identity Federation

111. Are all payments made according to the contract(s)?

112. Does the Identity Federation project have a Statement of Work?

113. Has appropriate allowance been made for the effect of the learning curve on all personnel joining the Identity Federation project who do not have the required prior industry, functional & technical expertise?

114. Does the implementation plan have an appropriate division of responsibilities?

115. Alignment to strategic goals & objectives?

116. What are the risks that could significantly affect the schedule of the Identity Federation project?

117. Pop quiz – what changed on Identity Federation project scope statement input?

118. Is there a scope management plan that includes how Identity Federation project scope will be defined, developed, monitored, validated and controlled?

119. What is the relative power of the Identity Federation project manager?

120. Is it possible to track all classes of Identity Federation project work (e.g. scheduled, un-scheduled, defect repair, etc.)?

121. Are non-critical path items updated and agreed upon with the teams?

122. Has a quality assurance plan been developed for the Identity Federation project?

123. Have you identified possible roadblocks?

124. During what part of the PM process is the Identity Federation project scope statement created?

125. Are changes in deliverable commitments agreed to by all affected groups & individuals?

126. Is there a formal set of procedures supporting Issues Management?

127. Are all resource assumptions documented?

128. Where do scope management processes fit in?

129. Organizational policies that might affect the availability of resources?

130. Do you secure formal approval of changes and requirements from stakeholders?

2.3 Requirements Management Plan: Identity Federation

131. Is it new or replacing an existing business system or process?

132. Why manage requirements?

133. Do you know which stakeholders will participate in the requirements effort?

134. Is requirements work dependent on any other specific Identity Federation project or non-Identity Federation project activities (e.g. funding, approvals, procurement)?

135. Who is responsible for monitoring and tracking the Identity Federation project requirements?

136. Do you really need to write this document at all?

137. Did you provide clear and concise specifications?

138. Who will finally present the work or product(s) for acceptance?

139. Do you have an appropriate arrangement for meetings?

140. Is infrastructure setup part of your Identity Federation project?

141. Do you expect stakeholders to be cooperative?

142. Are all the stakeholders ready for the transition into the user community?

143. Does the Identity Federation project have a Change Control process?

144. Have stakeholders been instructed in the Change Control process?

145. What is the earliest finish date for this Identity Federation project if it is scheduled to start on ...?

146. What went right?

147. Will you have access to stakeholders when you need them?

148. How will you develop the schedule of requirements activities?

149. The wbs is developed as part of a joint planning session. and how do you know that youhave done this right?

150. Did you use declarative statements?

2.4 Requirements Documentation: Identity Federation

151. How linear / iterative is your Requirements Gathering process (or will it be)?

152. Validity. does the system provide the functions which best support the customers needs?

153. How do you know when a Requirement is accurate enough?

154. Who is interacting with the system?

155. Who is involved?

156. Consistency. are there any requirements conflicts?

157. Is the requirement properly understood?

158. Do your constraints stand?

159. Can the requirement be changed without a large impact on other requirements?

160. Can you check system requirements?

161. Where are business rules being captured?

162. What are the attributes of a customer?

163. Completeness. are all functions required by the

customer included?

164. How does what is being described meet the business need?

165. Does the system provide the functions which best support the customers needs?

166. Verifiability. can the requirements be checked?

167. Is the requirement realistically testable?

168. Where do you define what is a customer, what are the attributes of customer?

169. Are there any requirements conflicts?

170. How will requirements be documented and who signs off on them?

2.5 Requirements Traceability Matrix: Identity Federation

171. Do you have a clear understanding of all subcontracts in place?

172. Why use a WBS?

173. Will you use a Requirements Traceability Matrix?

174. What are the chronologies, contingencies, consequences, criteria?

175. How will it affect the stakeholders personally in career?

176. What is the WBS?

177. Why do you manage scope?

178. How small is small enough?

179. Describe the process for approving requirements so they can be added to the traceability matrix and Identity Federation project work can be performed. Will the Identity Federation project requirements become approved in writing?

180. How do you manage scope?

181. Is there a requirements traceability process in place?

182. What percentage of Identity Federation projects are producing traceability matrices between requirements and other work products?

2.6 Project Scope Statement: Identity Federation

183. Elements of scope management that deal with concept development ?

184. Will the risk documents be filed?

185. What is the product of this Identity Federation project?

186. How often do you estimate that the scope might change, and why?

187. Relevant - ask yourself can you get there; why are you doing this Identity Federation project?

188. What is change?

189. Is this process communicated to the customer and team members?

190. Is there a baseline plan against which to measure progress?

191. Do you anticipate new stakeholders joining the Identity Federation project over time?

192. Is the Identity Federation project organization documented and on file?

193. Identify how your team and you will create the Identity Federation project scope statement and the

work breakdown structure (WBS). Document how you will create the Identity Federation project scope statement and WBS, and make sure you answer the following questions: In defining Identity Federation project scope and the WBS, will you and your Identity Federation project team be using methods defined by your organization, methods defined by the Identity Federation project management office (PMO), or other methods?

194. Will the Identity Federation project risks be managed according to the Identity Federation projects risk management process?

195. Is the plan under configuration management?

196. Are the input requirements from the team members clearly documented and communicated?

197. Will the risk plan be updated on a regular and frequent basis?

198. Does the scope statement still need some clarity?

199. What are the possible consequences should a risk come to occur?

200. Have the configuration management functions been assigned?

201. If there are vendors, have they signed off on the Identity Federation project Plan?

202. Will tasks be marked complete only after QA has been successfully completed?

2.7 Assumption and Constraint Log: Identity Federation

203. How many Identity Federation project staff does this specific process affect?

204. Is the current scope of the Identity Federation project substantially different than that originally defined in the approved Identity Federation project plan?

205. What do you audit?

206. If it is out of compliance, should the process be amended or should the Plan be amended?

207. What weaknesses do you have?

208. Does a documented Identity Federation project organizational policy & plan (i.e. governance model) exist?

209. Have the scope, objectives, costs, benefits and impacts been communicated to all involved and/or impacted stakeholders and work groups?

210. Does the traceability documentation describe the tool and/or mechanism to be used to capture traceability throughout the life cycle?

211. Are processes for release management of new development from coding and unit testing, to integration testing, to training, and production

defined and followed?

212. Are you meeting your customers expectations consistently?

213. Contradictory information between document sections?

214. Diagrams and tables are included to account for complex concepts and increase overall readability?

215. Are there standards for code development?

216. Does the document/deliverable meet all requirements (for example, statement of work) specific to this deliverable?

217. What other teams / processes would be impacted by changes to the current process, and how?

218. Does the Identity Federation project have a formal Identity Federation project Plan?

219. Are there ways to reduce the time it takes to get something approved?

220. Is the steering committee active in Identity Federation project oversight?

221. What strengths do you have?

2.8 Work Breakdown Structure: Identity Federation

222. How many levels?

223. Why would you develop a Work Breakdown Structure?

224. How far down?

225. How big is a work-package?

226. Do you need another level?

227. Who has to do it?

228. When does it have to be done?

229. What is the probability of completing the Identity Federation project in less that xx days?

230. Is it still viable?

231. Is it a change in scope?

232. Is the work breakdown structure (wbs) defined and is the scope of the Identity Federation project clear with assigned deliverable owners?

233. Where does it take place?

234. When do you stop?

235. How much detail?

236. Why is it useful?

237. What has to be done?

2.9 WBS Dictionary: Identity Federation

238. Are the contractors estimates of costs at completion reconcilable with cost data reported to us?

239. Appropriate work authorization documents which subdivide the contractual effort and responsibilities, within functional organizations?

240. The total budget for the contract (including estimates for authorized and unpriced work)?

241. Is subcontracted work defined and identified to the appropriate subcontractor within the proper WBS element?

242. Are overhead budgets and costs being handled according to the disclosure statement when applicable, or otherwise properly classified (for example, engineering overhead, IR&D)?

243. Is authorization of budgets in excess of the contract budget base controlled formally and done with the full knowledge and recognition of the procuring activity?

244. Are the bases and rates for allocating costs from each indirect pool to commercial work consistent with the already stated used to allocate corresponding costs to Government contracts?

245. Identify and isolate causes of favorable and unfavorable cost and schedule variances?

246. Does the sum of all work package budgets plus planning packages within control accounts equal the budgets assigned to the already stated control accounts?

247. Is all contract work included in the CWBS?

248. Are data being used by managers in an effective manner to ascertain Identity Federation project or functional status, to identify reasons or significant variance, and to initiate appropriate corrective action?

249. Budgeted cost for work performed?

250. Does the contractors system provide for determination of price variance by comparing planned Vs actual commitments?

251. Wbs elements contractually specified for reporting of status to you (lowest level only)?

252. Is the entire contract planned in time-phased control accounts to the extent practicable?

253. What should you drop in order to add something new?

254. Where engineering standards or other internal work measurement systems are used, is there a formal relationship between corresponding values and work package budgets?

255. Major functional areas of contract effort?

256. Is the work done on a work package level as described in the WBS dictionary?

257. Does the contractors system provide unit costs, equivalent unit or lot costs in terms of labor, material, other direct, and indirect costs?

2.10 Schedule Management Plan: Identity Federation

258. Are adequate resources provided for the quality assurance function?

259. What is the difference between % Complete and % work?

260. List all schedule constraints here. Must the Identity Federation project be complete by a specified date?

261. Are meeting minutes captured and sent out after the meeting?

262. Is it standard practice to formally commit stakeholders to the Identity Federation project via agreements?

263. Is a process defined to measure the performance of the schedule management process itself?

264. Why conduct schedule analysis?

265. Have all necessary approvals been obtained?

266. Is the quality assurance team identified?

267. Are there any activities or deliverables being added or gold-plated that could be dropped or scaled back without falling short of the original requirement?

268. Is there an onboarding process in place?

269. Have Identity Federation project success criteria been defined?

270. Are the payment terms being followed?

271. Has a provision been made to reassess Identity Federation project risks at various Identity Federation project stages?

272. Is there a procedure for management, control and release of schedule margin?

273. Are the predecessor and successor relationships accurate?

274. How are Identity Federation projects different from operations?

2.11 Activity List: Identity Federation

275. Where will it be performed?

276. How can the Identity Federation project be displayed graphically to better visualize the activities?

277. How detailed should a Identity Federation project get?

278. What went well?

279. Can you determine the activity that must finish, before this activity can start?

280. What are you counting on?

281. What is the probability the Identity Federation project can be completed in xx weeks?

282. What went wrong?

283. How should ongoing costs be monitored to try to keep the Identity Federation project within budget?

284. How do you determine the late start (LS) for each activity?

285. Is there anything planned that does not need to be here?

286. What will be performed?

287. Are the required resources available or need to

be acquired?

288. When do the individual activities need to start and finish?

289. When will the work be performed?

290. How much slack is available in the Identity Federation project?

291. Who will perform the work?

292. What did not go as well?

2.12 Activity Attributes: Identity Federation

293. How much activity detail is required?

294. How many days do you need to complete the work scope with a limit of X number of resources?

295. Have constraints been applied to the start and finish milestones for the phases?

296. How else could the items be grouped?

297. Resources to accomplish the work?

298. How do you manage time?

299. Activity: what is Missing?

300. Activity: fair or not fair?

301. Activity: what is In the Bag?

302. What is missing?

303. Does your organization of the data change its meaning?

304. Where else does it apply?

305. Have you identified the Activity Leveling Priority code value on each activity?

306. What conclusions/generalizations can you draw from this?

307. Time for overtime?

308. What is the general pattern here?

309. Can more resources be added?

2.13 Milestone List: Identity Federation

310. Level of the Innovation?

311. What date will the task finish?

312. Sustainable financial backing?

313. When will the Identity Federation project be complete?

314. Calculate how long can activity be delayed?

315. It is to be a narrative text providing the crucial aspects of your Identity Federation project proposal answering what, who, how, when and where?

316. How difficult will it be to do specific activities on this Identity Federation project?

317. How soon can the activity start?

318. Timescales, deadlines and pressures?

319. Continuity, supply chain robustness?

320. Sustaining internal capabilities?

321. Usps (unique selling points)?

322. How will the milestone be verified?

323. Do you foresee any technical risks or developmental challenges?

324. What has been done so far?

325. Loss of key staff?

326. What background experience, skills, and strengths does the team bring to your organization?

327. What is the market for your technology, product or service?

2.14 Network Diagram: Identity Federation

328. What activities must follow this activity?

329. What must be completed before an activity can be started?

330. Are you on time?

331. Can you calculate the confidence level?

332. Why must you schedule milestones, such as reviews, throughout the Identity Federation project?

333. Are the gantt chart and/or network diagram updated periodically and used to assess the overall Identity Federation project timetable?

334. What to do and When?

335. Which type of network diagram allows you to depict four types of dependencies?

336. What are the tools?

337. If a current contract exists, can you provide the vendor name, contract start, and contract expiration date?

338. How confident can you be in your milestone dates and the delivery date?

339. What is your organizations history in doing similar activities?

340. Where do you schedule uncertainty time?

341. What job or jobs precede it?

342. What are the Major Administrative Issues?

343. What activity must be completed immediately before this activity can start?

344. What is the probability of completing the Identity Federation project in less that xx days?

345. What job or jobs could run concurrently?

346. What controls the start and finish of a job?

2.15 Activity Resource Requirements: Identity Federation

347. How many signatures do you require on a check and does this match what is in your policy and procedures?

348. How do you handle petty cash?

349. Anything else?

350. Why do you do that?

351. What are constraints that you might find during the Human Resource Planning process?

352. Other support in specific areas?

353. Are there unresolved issues that need to be addressed?

354. Do you use tools like decomposition and rolling-wave planning to produce the activity list and other outputs?

355. When does monitoring begin?

356. What is the Work Plan Standard?

357. Which logical relationship does the PDM use most often?

2.16 Resource Breakdown Structure: Identity Federation

358. What is Identity Federation project communication management?

359. Who is allowed to perform which functions?

360. What is the primary purpose of the human resource plan?

361. What is the number one predictor of a groups productivity?

362. What defines a successful Identity Federation project?

363. Why is this important?

364. Why time management?

365. Which resource planning tool provides information on resource responsibility and accountability?

366. Any changes from stakeholders?

367. Who needs what information?

368. Who will use the system?

369. What is the purpose of assigning and documenting responsibility?

370. The list could probably go on, but, the thing that you would most like to know is, How long & How much?

371. Is predictive resource analysis being done?

372. What can you do to improve productivity?

2.17 Activity Duration Estimates: Identity Federation

373. Do procedures exist describing how the Identity Federation project scope will be managed?

374. Briefly summarize the work done by Maslow, Herzberg, McClellan, McGregor, Ouchi, Thamhain and Wilemon, and Covey. How do theories relate to Identity Federation project management?

375. Is the work performed reviewed against contractual objectives?

376. Why should Identity Federation project managers strive to make jobs look easy?

377. How does Identity Federation project integration management relate to the Identity Federation project life cycle, stakeholders, and the other Identity Federation project management knowledge areas?

378. Calculate the expected duration for an activity that has a most likely time of 5, a pessimistic time of 13, and a optimiztic time of 3?

379. Are processes defined to monitor Identity Federation project cost and schedule variances?

380. What is wrong with this scenario?

381. How much time is required to develop it?

382. Do checklists exist that list frequently performed activities?

383. Which type of mathematical analysis is being used?

384. How difficult will it be to complete specific activities on this Identity Federation project?

385. What is the difference between using brainstorming and the Delphi technique for risk identification?

386. How have experts such as Deming, Juran, Crosby, and Taguchi affected the quality movement and todays use of Six Sigma?

387. Is evaluation criteria defined to rate proposals?

388. Is earned value analysis completed to assess Identity Federation project performance?

389. Which is a benefit of an analogous Identity Federation project estimate?

390. Are tools and techniques defined for gathering, integrating and distributing Identity Federation project outputs?

391. Consider the changes in the job market for information technology workers. How does the job market and current state of the economy affect human resource management?

2.18 Duration Estimating Worksheet: Identity Federation

392. What is next?

393. How can the Identity Federation project be displayed graphically to better visualize the activities?

394. Does the Identity Federation project provide innovative ways for stakeholders to overcome obstacles or deliver better outcomes?

395. Value pocket identification & quantification what are value pockets?

396. When, then?

397. Is a construction detail attached (to aid in explanation)?

398. Will the Identity Federation project collaborate with the local community and leverage resources?

399. Small or large Identity Federation project?

400. What utility impacts are there?

401. What work will be included in the Identity Federation project?

402. For other activities, how much delay can be tolerated?

403. How should ongoing costs be monitored to try to keep the Identity Federation project within budget?

404. Is this operation cost effective?

405. Done before proceeding with this activity or what can be done concurrently?

406. When does your organization expect to be able to complete it?

407. Do any colleagues have experience with your organization and/or RFPs?

408. What info is needed?

2.19 Project Schedule: Identity Federation

409. Are quality inspections and review activities listed in the Identity Federation project schedule(s)?

410. How can you minimize or control changes to Identity Federation project schedules?

411. Are the original Identity Federation project schedule and budget realistic?

412. Why do you think schedule issues often cause the most conflicts on Identity Federation projects?

413. Why or why not?

414. Why do you need schedules?

415. Is the Identity Federation project schedule available for all Identity Federation project team members to review?

416. What is risk management?

417. What documents, if any, will the subcontractor provide (eg Identity Federation project schedule, quality plan etc)?

418. Master Identity Federation project schedule?

419. If there are any qualifying green components to this Identity Federation project, what portion of the

total Identity Federation project cost is green?

420. To what degree is do you feel the entire team was committed to the Identity Federation project schedule?

421. Your Identity Federation project management plan results in a Identity Federation project schedule that is too long. If the Identity Federation project network diagram cannot change and you have extra personnel resources, what is the BEST thing to do?

422. If you can not fix it, how do you do it differently?

423. Is there a Schedule Management Plan that establishes the criteria and activities for developing, monitoring and controlling the Identity Federation project schedule?

424. Change management required?

425. Month Identity Federation project take?

426. Are there activities that came from a template or previous Identity Federation project that are not applicable on this phase of this Identity Federation project?

2.20 Cost Management Plan: Identity Federation

427. Are target dates established for each milestone deliverable?

428. Is an industry recognized mechanized support tool(s) being used for Identity Federation project scheduling & tracking?

429. Are post milestone Identity Federation project reviews (PMPR) conducted with your organization at least once a year?

430. Are the appropriate IT resources adequate to meet planned commitments?

431. What threats might prevent you from getting there?

432. Are milestone deliverables effectively tracked and compared to Identity Federation project plan?

433. Does the detailed work plan match the complexity of tasks with the capabilities of personnel?

434. Is your organization certified as a supplier, wholesaler, regular dealer, or manufacturer of corresponding products/supplies?

435. Are schedule deliverables actually delivered?

436. Was your organizations estimating methodology

being used and followed?

437. What is your organizations history in doing similar tasks?

438. Similar Identity Federation projects?

439. Are tasks tracked by hours?

440. What is cost and Identity Federation project cost management?

441. What is the work breakdown structure for the Identity Federation project?

442. Are Identity Federation project team members involved in detailed estimating and scheduling?

443. Are internal Identity Federation project status meetings held at reasonable intervals?

2.21 Activity Cost Estimates: Identity Federation

444. Estimated cost?

445. What are you looking for?

446. What is the activity recast of the budget?

447. Were sponsors and decision makers available when needed outside regularly scheduled meetings?

448. Why do you manage cost?

449. What is the activity inventory?

450. Who determines when the contractor is paid?

451. Did the consultant work with local staff to develop local capacity?

452. How many activities should you have?

453. Does the activity rely on a common set of tools to carry it out?

454. Would you hire them again?

455. What skill level is required to do the job?

456. Is there anything unique in this Identity Federation projects scope statement that will affect resources?

457. Can you delete activities or make them inactive?

458. How do you treat administrative costs in the activity inventory?

459. Will you need to provide essential services information about activities?

460. How Award?

461. What is included in indirect cost being allocated?

2.22 Cost Estimating Worksheet: Identity Federation

462. Ask: are others positioned to know, are others credible, and will others cooperate?

463. What is the estimated labor cost today based upon this information?

464. Does the Identity Federation project provide innovative ways for stakeholders to overcome obstacles or deliver better outcomes?

465. What will others want?

466. How will the results be shared and to whom?

467. Will the Identity Federation project collaborate with the local community and leverage resources?

468. Can a trend be established from historical performance data on the selected measure and are the criteria for using trend analysis or forecasting methods met?

469. What costs are to be estimated?

470. What additional Identity Federation project(s) could be initiated as a result of this Identity Federation project?

471. Is it feasible to establish a control group arrangement?

472. Identify the timeframe necessary to monitor progress and collect data to determine how the selected measure has changed?

473. Is the Identity Federation project responsive to community need?

474. Who is best positioned to know and assist in identifying corresponding factors?

475. What is the purpose of estimating?

476. What happens to any remaining funds not used?

477. What can be included?

2.23 Cost Baseline: Identity Federation

478. Have the lessons learned been filed with the Identity Federation project Management Office?

479. Does the suggested change request seem to represent a necessary enhancement to the product?

480. Vac -variance at completion, how much over/ under budget do you expect to be?

481. Has the actual cost of the Identity Federation project (or Identity Federation project phase) been tallied and compared to the approved budget?

482. What would the life cycle costs be?

483. Where do changes come from?

484. Have all approved changes to the schedule baseline been identified and impact on the Identity Federation project documented?

485. Pcs for your new business. what would the life cycle costs be?

486. How long are you willing to wait before you find out were late?

487. How will cost estimates be used?

488. Verify business objectives. Are others

appropriate, and well-articulated?

489. What is cost and Identity Federation project cost management?

490. When should cost estimates be developed?

491. Are you asking management for something as a result of this update?

492. Does a process exist for establishing a cost baseline to measure Identity Federation project performance?

493. On time?

2.24 Quality Management Plan: Identity Federation

494. Who else should be involved ?

495. How long do you retain data?

496. What is the audience for the data?

497. Diagrams and tables to account for complex concepts and increase overall readability?

498. How are your organizations compensation and recognition approaches and the performance management system used to reinforce high performance?

499. How are senior leaders, employees, and your organization involved in supporting the community?

500. How do you measure?

501. What is the return on investment?

502. What are your organizations current levels and trends for the already stated measures related to customer satisfaction/ dissatisfaction and product/ service performance?

503. Do trained quality assurance auditors conduct the audits as defined in the Quality Management Plan and scheduled by the Identity Federation project manager?

504. What methods are used?

505. How is staff trained in procedures?

506. How does the material compare to a regulatory threshold?

507. Sampling part of task?

508. Is there a Quality Management Plan?

509. How do you ensure that your sampling methods and procedures meet your data needs?

510. What are the appropriate test methods to be used?

511. How do senior leaders review organizational performance?

512. How does your organization ensure the quality, reliability, and user-friendliness of its hardware and software?

2.25 Quality Metrics: Identity Federation

513. What level of statistical confidence do you use?

514. How should customers provide input?

515. Is the reporting frequency appropriate?

516. How are requirements conflicts resolved?

517. Where is quality now?

518. What can manufacturing professionals do to ensure quality is seen as an integral part of the entire product lifecycle?

519. Is there a set of procedures to capture, analyze and act on quality metrics?

520. Does risk analysis documentation meet standards?

521. Was the overall quality better or worse than previous products?

522. Was material distributed on time?

523. Is a risk containment plan in place?

524. How does one achieve stability?

525. Product Availability ?

526. When is the security analysis testing complete?

527. Did the team meet the Identity Federation project success criteria documented in the Quality Metrics Matrix?

528. How do you calculate corresponding metrics?

529. Are quality metrics defined?

530. What method of measurement do you use?

2.26 Process Improvement Plan: Identity Federation

531. What personnel are the coaches for your initiative?

532. Are you following the quality standards?

533. How do you manage quality?

534. Management commitment at all levels?

535. Does your process ensure quality?

536. Where do you want to be?

537. What makes people good SPI coaches?

538. Why do you want to achieve the goal?

539. Have storage and access mechanisms and procedures been determined?

540. Have the supporting tools been developed or acquired?

541. Where do you focus?

542. What lessons have you learned so far?

543. What personnel are the champions for the initiative?

544. Purpose of goal: the motive is determined by asking, why do you want to achieve this goal?

545. To elicit goal statements, do you ask a question such as, What do you want to achieve?

546. What is the test-cycle concept?

547. Who should prepare the process improvement action plan?

548. What actions are needed to address the problems and achieve the goals?

549. What personnel are the sponsors for that initiative?

2.27 Responsibility Assignment Matrix: Identity Federation

550. The already stated responsible for the establishment of budgets and assignment of resources for overhead performance?

551. Is the anticipated (firm and potential) business base Identity Federation projected in a rational, consistent manner?

552. Are the actual costs used for variance analysis reconcilable with data from the accounting system?

553. What are the known stakeholder requirements?

554. What materials and procurements needed?

555. Are all authorized tasks assigned to identified organizational elements?

556. Are all elements of indirect expense identified to overhead cost budgets of Identity Federation projections?

557. Are work packages assigned to performing organizations?

558. Are your organizations and items of cost assigned to each pool identified?

559. Are overhead cost budgets established for each organization which has authority to incur overhead

costs?

560. Changes in the nature of the overhead requirements?

561. Direct labor dollars and/or hours?

562. Ideas for developing soft skills at your organization?

563. Changes in the direct base to which overhead costs are allocated?

564. What expertise is not available in your department?

565. Who is going to do that work?

566. What cost control tool do many experts say is crucial to Identity Federation project management?

567. Wbs elements contractually specified for reporting of status (lowest level only)?

2.28 Roles and Responsibilities: Identity Federation

568. Are the quality assurance functions and related roles and responsibilities clearly defined?

569. Once the responsibilities are defined for the Identity Federation project, have the deliverables, roles and responsibilities been clearly communicated to every participant?

570. What specific behaviors did you observe?

571. Who: who is involved?

572. What should you do now to ensure that you are meeting all expectations of your current position?

573. Influence: what areas of organizational decision making are you able to influence when you do not have authority to make the final decision?

574. Are Identity Federation project team roles and responsibilities identified and documented?

575. To decide whether to use a quality measurement, ask how will you know when it is achieved?

576. Does the team have access to and ability to use data analysis tools?

577. Do the values and practices inherent in the culture of your organization foster or hinder the

process?

578. What is working well?

579. Are governance roles and responsibilities documented?

580. Are Identity Federation project team roles and responsibilities identified and documented?

581. Have you ever been a part of this team?

582. Accountabilities: what are the roles and responsibilities of individual team members?

583. Does your vision/mission support a culture of quality data?

584. Was the expectation clearly communicated?

585. Authority: what areas/Identity Federation projects in your work do you have the authority to decide upon and act on the already stated decisions?

586. What expectations were met?

2.29 Human Resource Management Plan: Identity Federation

587. Have Identity Federation project management standards and procedures been identified / established and documented?

588. Have the procedures for identifying budget variances been followed?

589. Are Identity Federation project contact logs kept up to date?

590. Does the resource management plan include a personnel development plan?

591. What were things that you did very well and want to do the same again on the next Identity Federation project?

592. Sensitivity analysis?

593. Are internal Identity Federation project status meetings held at reasonable intervals?

594. Has the scope management document been updated and distributed to help prevent scope creep?

595. Are enough systems & user personnel assigned to the Identity Federation project?

596. Are the people assigned to the Identity Federation project sufficiently qualified?

597. Are mitigation strategies identified?

598. Are people being developed to meet the challenges of the future?

599. Do you have the reasons why the changes to your organizational systems and capabilities are required?

600. Did the Identity Federation project team have the right skills?

601. Is there any form of automated support for Issues Management?

602. Is pert / critical path or equivalent methodology being used?

603. Is the Identity Federation project schedule available for all Identity Federation project team members to review?

604. Quality assurance overheads?

605. Who is evaluated?

2.30 Communications Management Plan: Identity Federation

606. Which stakeholders can influence others?

607. How is this initiative related to other portfolios, programs, or Identity Federation projects?

608. Timing: when do the effects of the communication take place?

609. What is the stakeholders level of authority?

610. Which team member will work with each stakeholder?

611. Is there an important stakeholder who is actively opposed and will not receive messages?

612. Who is responsible?

613. What approaches do you use?

614. Will messages be directly related to the release strategy or phases of the Identity Federation project?

615. Who did you turn to if you had questions?

616. What does the stakeholder need from the team?

617. What steps can you take for a positive relationship?

618. Which stakeholders are thought leaders, influences, or early adopters?

619. Are the stakeholders getting the information others need, are others consulted, are concerns addressed?

620. Are you constantly rushing from meeting to meeting?

621. What are the interrelationships?

622. How did the term stakeholder originate?

623. What communications method?

624. Who will use or be affected by the result of a Identity Federation project?

2.31 Risk Management Plan: Identity Federation

625. What can you do to minimize the impact if it does?

626. What would you do?

627. How do you manage Identity Federation project Risk?

628. Do the requirements require the creation of components that are unlike anything your organization has previously built?

629. What other risks are created by choosing an avoidance strategy?

630. Are tool mentors available?

631. How well were you able to manage your risk before?

632. Are formal technical reviews part of this process?

633. Technology risk: is the Identity Federation project technically feasible?

634. Are the reports useful and easy to read?

635. How is the audit profession changing?

636. Why do you need to manage Identity Federation

project Risk?

637. Do you have a mechanism for managing change?

638. Is there additional information that would make you more confident about your analysis?

639. Anticipated volatility of the requirements?

640. Which risks should get the attention?

641. Maximize short-term return on investment?

642. Are status updates being made on schedule and are the updates clearly described?

643. Why do you want risk management?

2.32 Risk Register: Identity Federation

644. When is it going to be done?

645. Recovery actions - planned actions taken once a risk has occurred to allow you to move on. What should you do after?

646. Who is accountable?

647. Are your objectives at risk?

648. What are the major risks facing the Identity Federation project?

649. What is a Risk?

650. What is the probability and impact of the risk occurring?

651. How are risks graded?

652. People risk -are people with appropriate skills available to help complete the Identity Federation project?

653. Risk categories: what are the main categories of risks that should be addressed on this Identity Federation project?

654. What may happen or not go according to plan?

655. What are your key risks/show istoppers and what is being done to manage them?

656. Are implemented controls working as others should?

657. What are the assumptions and current status that support the assessment of the risk?

658. What evidence do you have to justify the likelihood score of the risk (audit, incident report, claim, complaints, inspection, internal review)?

659. What could prevent you delivering on the strategic program objectives and what is being done to mitigate corresponding issues?

660. How could corresponding Risk affect the Identity Federation project in terms of cost and schedule?

661. What is your current and future risk profile?

662. Who needs to know about this?

2.33 Probability and Impact Assessment: Identity Federation

663. What should be the requirement of organizational restructuring as each subIdentity Federation project goes through a different lifecycle phase?

664. Is a software Identity Federation project management tool available?

665. What are the chances the event will occur?

666. Is the technology to be built new to your organization?

667. Are the risk data complete?

668. Do end-users have realistic expectations?

669. How would you suggest monitoring for risk transition indicators?

670. Which risks need to move on to Perform Quantitative Risk Analysis?

671. What are the current demands of the customer?

672. Does the customer understand the software process?

673. Workarounds are determined during which step of risk management?

674. Does the customer have a solid idea of what is required?

675. How completely has the customer been identified?

676. Are there new risks that mitigation strategies might introduce?

677. How will economic events and trends likely affect the Identity Federation project?

678. How do you define a risk?

679. What will be the environmental impact of the Identity Federation project?

680. Risk categorization -which of your categories has more risk than others?

681. Sensitivity analysis -which risks will have the most impact on the Identity Federation project?

682. What can you do about it?

2.34 Probability and Impact Matrix: Identity Federation

683. Workarounds are determined during which risk management process?

684. Which is the BEST thing to do?

685. Do you need a risk management plan?

686. Several experts are offsite, and wish to be included. How can this be done?

687. My Identity Federation project leader has suddenly left your organization, what do you do?

688. Has the need for the Identity Federation project been properly established?

689. How are you working with risks?

690. What can possibly go wrong?

691. The customer requests a change to the Identity Federation project that would increase the Identity Federation project risk. Which should you do before ass the others?

692. Do you use any methods to analyze risks?

693. Do others match with the clients requirement?

694. Is the process supported by tools?

695. Premium on reliability of product?

696. Is the present organizational structure for handling the Identity Federation project sufficient?

697. Do the requirements require the creation of new algorithms?

698. Is the customer willing to establish rapid communication links with the developer?

699. Will there be an increase in the political conservatism?

700. Costs associated with late delivery or a defective product?

2.35 Risk Data Sheet: Identity Federation

701. What are your core values?

702. What can happen?

703. What if client refuses?

704. Do effective diagnostic tests exist?

705. What are you here for (Mission)?

706. What are you trying to achieve (Objectives)?

707. How do you handle product safely?

708. Risk of what?

709. Is the data sufficiently specified in terms of the type of failure being analyzed, and its frequency or probability?

710. What are you weak at and therefore need to do better?

711. What was measured?

712. What do you know?

713. Whom do you serve (customers)?

714. Potential for recurrence?

715. What actions can be taken to eliminate or remove risk?

716. How can it happen?

717. How reliable is the data source?

718. Has a sensitivity analysis been carried out?

719. What are the main opportunities available to you that you should grab while you can?

720. What can you do?

2.36 Procurement Management Plan: Identity Federation

721. Public engagement – did you get it right?

722. How will you coordinate Procurement with aspects of the Identity Federation project?

723. Specific - is the objective clear in terms of what, how, when, and where the situation will be changed?

724. Were Identity Federation project team members involved in detailed estimating and scheduling?

725. Are risk oriented checklists used during risk identification?

726. Is there a set of procedures defining the scope, procedures, and deliverables defining quality control?

727. Are written status reports provided on a designated frequent basis?

728. Are key risk mitigation strategies added to the Identity Federation project schedule?

729. Does all Identity Federation project documentation reside in a common repository for easy access?

730. What is a Identity Federation project Management Plan?

731. Have external dependencies been captured in the schedule?

732. Are updated Identity Federation project time & resource estimates reasonable based on the current Identity Federation project stage?

733. Have the key functions and capabilities been defined and assigned to each release or iteration?

734. Are the people assigned to the Identity Federation project sufficiently qualified?

735. Are meeting minutes captured and sent out after meetings?

736. Are software metrics formally captured, analyzed and used as a basis for other Identity Federation project estimates?

737. Is a payment system in place with proper reviews and approvals?

738. Are the quality tools and methods identified in the Quality Plan appropriate to the Identity Federation project?

2.37 Source Selection Criteria: Identity Federation

739. How should the solicitation aspects regarding past performance be structured?

740. Do you want to have them collaborate at subfactor level?

741. Are resultant proposal revisions allowed?

742. How are oral presentations documented?

743. Can you identify proposed teaming partners and/or subcontractors and consider the nature and extent of proposed involvement in satisfying the Identity Federation project requirements?

744. What does a sample rating scale look like?

745. What should be considered when developing evaluation standards?

746. What should clarifications include?

747. In order of importance, which evaluation criteria are the most critical to the determination of your overall rating?

748. What procedures are followed when a contractor requires access to classified information or a significant quantity of special material/information?

749. Will the technical evaluation factor unnecessarily force the acquisition into a higher-priced market segment?

750. What information may not be provided?

751. Do proposed hours support content and schedule?

752. Do you ensure you evaluate what you asked for, not what you want to see or expect to see?

753. When and what information can be considered with offerors regarding past performance?

754. How important is cost in the source selection decision relative to past performance and technical considerations?

755. Is a letter of commitment from each proposed team member and key subcontractor included?

756. What should be considered?

757. What should communications be used to accomplish?

758. How much weight should be placed on past performance information?

2.38 Stakeholder Management Plan: Identity Federation

759. Is the Identity Federation project sponsor clearly communicating the business case or rationale for why this Identity Federation project is needed?

760. Is stakeholder involvement adequate?

761. Does the Identity Federation project have a Quality Culture?

762. Where does the information come from?

763. Have process improvement efforts been completed before requirements efforts begin?

764. What are the criteria for selecting other suppliers, including subcontractors?

765. What is meant by managing the triple constraint?

766. Has a structured approach been used to break work effort into manageable components (WBS)?

767. What potential impact does the stakeholder have on the Identity Federation project?

768. Who will perform the review(s)?

769. Are corrective actions and variances reported?

770. Has the Identity Federation project manager

been identified?

771. Is the current scope of the Identity Federation project substantially different than that originally defined?

772. Can you perform this task or activity in a more effective manner?

773. Are regulatory inspections considered part of quality control?

774. Was trending evident between audits?

2.39 Change Management Plan: Identity Federation

775. How does the principle of senders and receivers make the Identity Federation project communications effort more complex?

776. What risks may occur upfront?

777. Will the culture embrace or reject this change?

778. What are the major changes to processes?

779. Have the approved procedures and policies been published?

780. Is it the same for each of the business units?

781. Who should be involved in developing a change management strategy?

782. What work practices will be affected?

783. What is the most positive interpretation it can receive?

784. Who might be able to help you the most?

785. Is a training information sheet available?

786. Will a different work structure focus people on what is important?

787. Has the training provider been established?

788. Who will fund the training?

789. What relationships will change?

790. Who will do the training?

791. What are the training strategies?

792. How frequently should you repeat the message?

793. What does a resilient organization look like?

3.0 Executing Process Group: Identity Federation

794. What are the Identity Federation project management deliverables of each process group?

795. Is the program supported by national and/or local organizations?

796. Contingency planning. if a risk event occurs, what will you do?

797. What type of people would you want on your team?

798. How can your organization use a weighted decision matrix to evaluate proposals as part of source selection?

799. How can you use Microsoft Identity Federation project and Excel to assist in Identity Federation project risk management?

800. Who will be the main sponsor?

801. Based on your Identity Federation project communication management plan, what worked well?

802. Why should Identity Federation project managers strive to make jobs look easy?

803. How is Identity Federation project performance

information created and distributed?

804. What are crucial elements of successful Identity Federation project plan execution?

805. Are the necessary foundations in place to ensure the sustainability of the results of the programme?

806. What are deliverables of your Identity Federation project?

807. What is in place for ensuring adequate change control on Identity Federation projects that involve outside contracts?

808. Is activity definition the first process involved in Identity Federation project time management?

809. What are the main types of goods and services being outsourced?

810. How will you know you did it?

811. What areas does the group agree are the biggest success on the Identity Federation project?

812. How well did the team follow the chosen processes?

813. What communication items need improvement?

3.1 Team Member Status Report: Identity Federation

814. Does the product, good, or service already exist within your organization?

815. Why is it to be done?

816. How will resource planning be done?

817. The problem with Reward & Recognition Programs is that the truly deserving people all too often get left out. How can you make it practical?

818. Are the products of your organizations Identity Federation projects meeting customers objectives?

819. Does your organization have the means (staff, money, contract, etc.) to produce or to acquire the product, good, or service?

820. Is there evidence that staff is taking a more professional approach toward management of your organizations Identity Federation projects?

821. What specific interest groups do you have in place?

822. Does every department have to have a Identity Federation project Manager on staff?

823. Will the staff do training or is that done by a third party?

824. How much risk is involved?

825. Are your organizations Identity Federation projects more successful over time?

826. Do you have an Enterprise Identity Federation project Management Office (EPMO)?

827. What is to be done?

828. How does this product, good, or service meet the needs of the Identity Federation project and your organization as a whole?

829. Are the attitudes of staff regarding Identity Federation project work improving?

830. When a teams productivity and success depend on collaboration and the efficient flow of information, what generally fails them?

831. How can you make it practical?

832. How it is to be done?

3.2 Change Request: Identity Federation

833. What is the change request log?

834. How are changes graded and who is responsible for the rating?

835. How do you get changes (code) out in a timely manner?

836. What should be regulated in a change control operating instruction?

837. How well do experienced software developers predict software change?

838. Are there requirements attributes that are strongly related to the complexity and size?

839. How can you ensure that changes have been made properly?

840. For which areas does this operating procedure apply?

841. Will new change requests be acknowledged in a timely manner?

842. What is the relationship between requirements attributes and attributes like complexity and size?

843. What can be filed?

844. Has your address changed?

845. Why were your requested changes rejected or not made?

846. Will all change requests and current status be logged?

847. How is quality being addressed on the Identity Federation project?

848. Have all related configuration items been properly updated?

849. When do you create a change request?

850. Can you answer what happened, who did it, when did it happen, and what else will be affected?

851. Will this change conflict with other requirements changes (e.g., lead to conflicting operational scenarios)?

852. What is the relationship between requirements attributes and reliability?

3.3 Change Log: Identity Federation

853. Is the change request open, closed or pending?

854. How does this change affect scope?

855. Should a more thorough impact analysis be conducted?

856. Is this a mandatory replacement?

857. Who initiated the change request?

858. Is the change request within Identity Federation project scope?

859. Does the suggested change request represent a desired enhancement to the products functionality?

860. Is the requested change request a result of changes in other Identity Federation project(s)?

861. How does this relate to the standards developed for specific business processes?

862. When was the request submitted?

863. Will the Identity Federation project fail if the change request is not executed?

864. Is the submitted change a new change or a modification of a previously approved change?

865. Do the described changes impact on the

integrity or security of the system?

866. When was the request approved?

867. Is the change backward compatible without limitations?

868. How does this change affect the timeline of the schedule?

3.4 Decision Log: Identity Federation

869. How do you know when you are achieving it?

870. How consolidated and comprehensive a story can you tell by capturing currently available incident data in a central location and through a log of key decisions during an incident?

871. What alternatives/risks were considered?

872. What is the line where eDiscovery ends and document review begins?

873. Who will be given a copy of this document and where will it be kept?

874. Decision-making process; how will the team make decisions?

875. How does an increasing emphasis on cost containment influence the strategies and tactics used?

876. Do strategies and tactics aimed at less than full control reduce the costs of management or simply shift the cost burden?

877. What eDiscovery problem or issue did your organization set out to fix or make better?

878. How does provision of information, both in terms of content and presentation, influence acceptance of alternative strategies?

879. Does anything need to be adjusted?

880. Which variables make a critical difference?

881. What is your overall strategy for quality control / quality assurance procedures?

882. Linked to original objective?

883. What was the rationale for the decision?

884. At what point in time does loss become unacceptable?

885. With whom was the decision shared or considered?

886. What are the cost implications?

887. Who is the decisionmaker?

888. How does the use a Decision Support System influence the strategies/tactics or costs?

3.5 Quality Audit: Identity Federation

889. How does your organization know that its system for inducting new staff to maximize workplace contributions are appropriately effective and constructive?

890. How well do you think your organization engages with the outside community?

891. How does your organization know that it is maintaining a conducive staff climate?

892. What review processes are in place for your organizations major activities?

893. How does your organization know that its system for recruiting the best staff possible are appropriately effective and constructive?

894. How does your organization know that the range and quality of its accommodation, catering and transportation services are appropriately effective and constructive?

895. Are all complaints involving the possible failure of a device, labeling, or packaging to meet any of its specifications reviewed, evaluated, and investigated?

896. Are all employees made aware of device defects which may occur from the improper performance of specific jobs?

897. Are there sufficient personnel having the

necessary education, background, training, and experience to assure that all operations are correctly performed?

898. How does your organization know that its system for ensuring that its training activities are appropriately resourced and support is appropriately effective and constructive?

899. How does your organization know that its system for staff performance planning and review is appropriately effective and constructive?

900. How does your organization ensure that equipment is appropriately maintained and producing valid results?

901. Is your organizations resource allocation system properly aligned with its collection of intentions?

902. Are training programs documented?

903. How does your organization know that the range and quality of its social and recreational services and facilities are appropriately effective and constructive in meeting the needs of staff?

904. What are you trying to accomplish with this audit?

905. Are complaint files maintained?

906. How does your organization know that its management system is appropriately effective and constructive?

907. Is your organizational structure a help or a hindrance to deployment?

908. Why are you trying to do it?

3.6 Team Directory: Identity Federation

909. Who will be the stakeholders on your next Identity Federation project?

910. Have you decided when to celebrate the Identity Federation projects completion date?

911. When does information need to be distributed?

912. How will the team handle changes?

913. How do unidentified risks impact the outcome of the Identity Federation project?

914. Days from the time the issue is identified?

915. What needs to be communicated?

916. Process decisions: are all start-up, turn over and close out requirements of the contract satisfied?

917. Contract requirements complied with?

918. Process decisions: do invoice amounts match accepted work in place?

919. Who are your stakeholders (customers, sponsors, end users, team members)?

920. Does a Identity Federation project team directory list all resources assigned to the Identity Federation

project?

921. Process decisions: are there any statutory or regulatory issues relevant to the timely execution of work?

922. How and in what format should information be presented?

923. Decisions: what could be done better to improve the quality of the constructed product?

924. Why is the work necessary?

925. When will you produce deliverables?

926. Who will talk to the customer?

927. Who should receive information (all stakeholders)?

3.7 Team Operating Agreement: Identity Federation

928. Do you listen for voice tone and word choice to understand the meaning behind words?

929. Communication protocols: how will the team communicate?

930. Resource allocation: how will individual team members account for time and expenses, and how will this be allocated in the team budget?

931. What are the boundaries (organizational or geographic) within which you operate?

932. How will you divide work equitably?

933. Is compensation based on team and individual performance?

934. Reimbursements: how will the team members be reimbursed for expenses and time commitments?

935. Do team members reside in more than two countries?

936. Do you ensure that all participants know how to use the required technology?

937. Do you solicit member feedback about meetings and what would make them better?

938. Are there influences outside the team that may affect performance, and if so, have you identified and addressed them?

939. What is teaming?

940. What is the number of cases currently teamed?

941. Has the appropriate access to relevant data and analysis capability been granted?

942. How will group handle unplanned absences?

943. Do team members need to frequently communicate as a full group to make timely decisions?

944. Have you set the goals and objectives of the team?

945. How does teaming fit in with overall organizational goals and meet organizational needs?

946. What is a Virtual Team?

947. To whom do you deliver your services?

3.8 Team Performance Assessment: Identity Federation

948. Do you promptly inform members about major developments that may affect them?

949. To what degree are sub-teams possible or necessary?

950. To what degree can team members vigorously define the teams purpose in considerations with others who are not part of the functioning team?

951. To what degree do team members feel that the purpose of the team is important, if not exciting?

952. To what degree do team members agree with the goals, relative importance, and the ways in which achievement will be measured?

953. To what degree does the teams work approach provide opportunity for members to engage in results-based evaluation?

954. How does Identity Federation project termination impact Identity Federation project team members?

955. Delaying market entry: how long is too long?

956. To what degree does the teams approach to its work allow for modification and improvement over time?

957. Can team performance be reliably measured in simulator and live exercises using the same assessment tool?

958. To what degree will team members, individually and collectively, commit time to help themselves and others learn and develop skills?

959. Can familiarity breed backup?

960. How hard do you try to make a good selection?

961. To what degree do the goals specify concrete team work products?

962. How do you manage human resources?

963. Social categorization and intergroup behaviour: Does minimal intergroup discrimination make social identity more positive?

964. Do you give group members authority to make at least some important decisions?

965. What do you think is the most constructive thing that could be done now to resolve considerations and disputes about method variance?

966. What is method variance?

967. To what degree will new and supplemental skills be introduced as the need is recognized?

3.9 Team Member Performance Assessment: Identity Federation

968. Can your organization rate by exception and assume that most employees are performing at an acceptable level?

969. Why were corresponding selected?

970. Why do performance reviews?

971. What are acceptable governance changes?

972. To what degree do members articulate the goals beyond the team membership?

973. To what extent did the evaluation influence the instructional path, such as with adaptive testing?

974. What types of learning are targeted (e.g., cognitive, affective, psychomotor, procedural)?

975. To what degree does the teams purpose contain themes that are particularly meaningful and memorable?

976. How was the determination made for which training platforms would be used (i.e., media selection)?

977. What, if any, steps are available for employees who feel they have been unfairly or inaccurately rated?

978. To what degree do all members feel responsible for all agreed-upon measures?

979. How effective is training that is delivered through technology-based platforms?

980. To what extent are systems and applications (e.g., game engine, mobile device platform) utilized?

981. How are performance measures and associated incentives developed?

982. How are evaluation results utilized?

983. Are there any safeguards to prevent intentional or unintentional rating errors?

984. How is assessment information achieved, stored?

985. What are the evaluation strategies (e.g., reaction, learning, behavior, results) used. What evaluation results did you have?

986. How are assessments designed, delivered, and otherwise used to maximize training?

987. New skills/knowledge gained this year?

3.10 Issue Log: Identity Federation

988. Who reported the issue?

989. What approaches to you feel are the best ones to use?

990. Is the issue log kept in a safe place?

991. How much time does it take to do it?

992. What effort will a change need?

993. What help do you and your team need from the stakeholders?

994. What is a change?

995. What is the status of the issue?

996. Why not more evaluators?

997. Do you feel more overwhelmed by stakeholders?

998. Persistence; will users learn a work around or will they be bothered every time?

999. What is the impact on the Business Case?

1000. Who is involved as you identify stakeholders?

1001. What are the stakeholders interrelationships?

1002. How is this initiative related to other portfolios,

programs, or Identity Federation projects?

1003. What is the impact on the risks?

1004. Are the stakeholders getting the information they need, are they consulted, are concerns addressed?

1005. How were past initiatives successful?

4.0 Monitoring and Controlling Process Group: Identity Federation

1006. Did it work?

1007. What input will you be required to provide the Identity Federation project team?

1008. Is the program in place as intended?

1009. How should needs be met?

1010. How many potential communications channels exist on the Identity Federation project?

1011. What is the expected monetary value of the Identity Federation project?

1012. Who are the Identity Federation project stakeholders?

1013. Are there areas that need improvement?

1014. Mitigate. what will you do to minimize the impact should a risk event occur?

1015. What is the timeline for the Identity Federation project?

1016. Use: how will they use the information?

1017. Is there undesirable impact on staff or resources?

1018. Did the Identity Federation project team have the right skills?

1019. Based on your Identity Federation project communication management plan, what worked well?

1020. What will you do to minimize the impact should a risk event occur?

1021. Propriety: who needs to be involved in the evaluation to be ethical?

1022. What are the deliverables?

1023. Is there adequate validation on required fields?

4.1 Project Performance Report: Identity Federation

1024. To what degree does the team possess adequate membership to achieve its ends?

1025. To what degree will the team adopt a concrete, clearly understood, and agreed-upon approach that will result in achievement of the teams goals?

1026. To what degree can team members meet frequently enough to accomplish the teams ends?

1027. To what degree does the information network communicate information relevant to the task?

1028. To what degree does the information network provide individuals with the information they require?

1029. To what degree is the team cognizant of small wins to be celebrated along the way?

1030. To what degree do individual skills and abilities match task demands?

1031. To what degree does the informal organization make use of individual resources and meet individual needs?

1032. To what degree does the funding match the requirement?

1033. To what degree are the structures of the formal

organization consistent with the behaviors in the informal organization?

1034. How will procurement be coordinated with other Identity Federation project aspects, such as scheduling and performance reporting?

1035. Next Steps?

1036. To what degree will the team ensure that all members equitably share the work essential to the success of the team?

1037. To what degree do team members understand one anothers roles and skills?

1038. To what degree are the members clear on what they are individually responsible for and what they are jointly responsible for?

4.2 Variance Analysis: Identity Federation

1039. Are management actions taken to reduce indirect costs when there are significant adverse variances?

1040. What was the cause of the increase in costs?

1041. Is work properly classified as measured effort, LOE, or apportioned effort and appropriately separated?

1042. How does your organization allocate the cost of shared expenses and services?

1043. Are procedures for variance analysis documented and consistently applied at the control account level and selected WBS and organizational levels at least monthly as a routine task?

1044. What is the performance to date and material commitment?

1045. Did your organization lose existing customers and/or gain new customers?

1046. Is the market likely to continue to grow at this rate next year?

1047. Did an existing competitor change strategy?

1048. Why are standard cost systems used?

1049. What business event caused the fluctuation?

1050. What does a favorable labor efficiency variance mean?

1051. Does the contractor use objective results, design reviews and tests to trace schedule performance?

1052. Are all elements of indirect expense identified to overhead cost budgets of Identity Federation projections?

1053. Who is generally responsible for monitoring and taking action on variances?

1054. What causes selling price variance?

1055. Historical experience?

1056. Are material costs reported within the same period as that in which BCWP is earned for that material?

1057. Are the overhead pools formally and adequately identified?

4.3 Earned Value Status: Identity Federation

1058. Are you hitting your Identity Federation projects targets?

1059. Validation is a process of ensuring that the developed system will actually achieve the stakeholders desired outcomes; Are you building the right product? What do you validate?

1060. Where is evidence-based earned value in your organization reported?

1061. How much is it going to cost by the finish?

1062. How does this compare with other Identity Federation projects?

1063. Verification is a process of ensuring that the developed system satisfies the stakeholders agreements and specifications; Are you building the product right? What do you verify?

1064. What is the unit of forecast value?

1065. Earned value can be used in almost any Identity Federation project situation and in almost any Identity Federation project environment. it may be used on large Identity Federation projects, medium sized Identity Federation projects, tiny Identity Federation projects (in cut-down form), complex and simple Identity Federation projects and in any market sector. some people, of course, know all about earned value, they have used it for years - but perhaps not as effectively as they could have?

1066. When is it going to finish?

1067. Where are your problem areas?

1068. If earned value management (EVM) is so good in determining the true status of a Identity Federation project and Identity Federation project its completion, why is it that hardly any one uses it in information systems related Identity Federation projects?

4.4 Risk Audit: Identity Federation

1069. Are all participants informed of safety issues?

1070. Improving fraud detection: do auditors react to abnormal inconsistencies between financial and non-financial measures?

1071. Do staff understand the extent of duty of care?

1072. Have reasonable steps been taken to reduce the risks to acceptable levels?

1073. Is there a clear procedure for reporting accidents/injuries?

1074. What does monitoring consist of?

1075. Do industry specialists and business risk auditors enhance audit reporting accuracy?

1076. Level of preparation and skill?

1077. Are enough people available?

1078. Does your organization have or has considered the need for insurance covers: public liability, professional indemnity and directors and officers liability?

1079. Is all expenditure authorised through an identified process?

1080. Does the Identity Federation project team have

experience with the technology to be implemented?

1081. What are the legal implications of not identifying a complete universe of business risks?

1082. Does the adoption of a business risk audit approach change internal control documentation and testing practices?

1083. What are the commonly used work arounds in high risk areas?

1084. What impact does prior experience have on decisions made during the risk-assessment process?

1085. Do you promote education and training opportunities?

1086. What are the costs associated with late delivery or a defective product?

4.5 Contractor Status Report: Identity Federation

1087. Describe how often regular updates are made to the proposed solution. Are corresponding regular updates included in the standard maintenance plan?

1088. How does the proposed individual meet each requirement?

1089. If applicable; describe your standard schedule for new software version releases. Are new software version releases included in the standard maintenance plan?

1090. What is the average response time for answering a support call?

1091. What was the overall budget or estimated cost?

1092. What was the actual budget or estimated cost for your organizations services?

1093. Who can list a Identity Federation project as organization experience, your organization or a previous employee of your organization?

1094. What was the budget or estimated cost for your organizations services?

1095. Are there contractual transfer concerns?

1096. How is risk transferred?

1097. What are the minimum and optimal bandwidth requirements for the proposed solution?

1098. How long have you been using the services?

1099. What process manages the contracts?

1100. What was the final actual cost?

4.6 Formal Acceptance: Identity Federation

1101. Was business value realized?

1102. Have all comments been addressed?

1103. Was the sponsor/customer satisfied?

1104. What are the requirements against which to test, Who will execute?

1105. What lessons were learned about your Identity Federation project management methodology?

1106. Was the client satisfied with the Identity Federation project results?

1107. What features, practices, and processes proved to be strengths or weaknesses?

1108. Was the Identity Federation project goal achieved?

1109. Do you buy pre-configured systems or build your own configuration?

1110. Who supplies data?

1111. Did the Identity Federation project achieve its MOV?

1112. General estimate of the costs and times to

complete the Identity Federation project?

1113. Is formal acceptance of the Identity Federation project product documented and distributed?

1114. What can you do better next time?

1115. What is the Acceptance Management Process?

1116. What function(s) does it fill or meet?

1117. How well did the team follow the methodology?

1118. Was the Identity Federation project managed well?

1119. Did the Identity Federation project manager and team act in a professional and ethical manner?

1120. How does your team plan to obtain formal acceptance on your Identity Federation project?

5.0 Closing Process Group: Identity Federation

1121. How well did the chosen processes fit the needs of the Identity Federation project?

1122. What is the overall risk of the Identity Federation project to your organization?

1123. What were things that you need to improve?

1124. Was the user/client satisfied with the end product?

1125. Is the Identity Federation project funded?

1126. What is the Identity Federation project name and date of completion?

1127. What do you need to do?

1128. What was learned?

1129. Were the outcomes different from the already stated planned?

1130. Based on your Identity Federation project communication management plan, what worked well?

1131. How dependent is the Identity Federation project on other Identity Federation projects or work efforts?

1132. Are there funding or time constraints?

1133. What were things that you did very well and want to do the same again on the next Identity Federation project?

1134. What is the risk of failure to your organization?

1135. Can the lesson learned be replicated?

1136. What could have been improved?

1137. What areas were overlooked on this Identity Federation project?

5.1 Procurement Audit: Identity Federation

1138. Were products/services not received within the prescribed time limit?

1139. Is funding made available for payments under the contract at the appropriate time and in accordance with the relevant national/public financial procedures?

1140. Is there any objection?

1141. Is procurement execution duly monitored and documented?

1142. Is data securely stored?

1143. Is there a form specified for bids?

1144. Are advantages and disadvantages of in-house production, outsourcing and Public Private Partnerships considered?

1145. When tenders were actually rejected because they were abnormally low, were reasons for this decision given and were they sufficiently grounded?

1146. Are proper financing arrangements taken?

1147. Does the procurement function/unit have the ability to apply electronic procurement?

1148. Is there a policy covering the relationship of other departments with vendors?

1149. Do at least two people have custodial responsibilities for negotiable checks (one checking on the other)?

1150. Where applicable, did your organization adequately manage experts employed to assist in the procurement process?

1151. Are there appropriate controls in place to ensure that procurement complies with the relevant legislation?

1152. Are budget transfers within the general fund made for only the already stated items permitted by law and regulation?

1153. Are the financial and business records of your organization stored in a secure fire resistant place?

1154. Is the routing of copies of purchase order forms defined?

1155. Was suitability of candidates accurately assessed?

1156. In a competitive dialogue, were solutions proposed or confidential information given by a candidate not revealed to others without his/her express agreement?

1157. Where funding is being arranged by borrowings, do corresponding have the necessary approval and legal authority?

5.2 Contract Close-Out: Identity Federation

1158. What is capture management?

1159. How does it work?

1160. Have all acceptance criteria been met prior to final payment to contractors?

1161. Has each contract been audited to verify acceptance and delivery?

1162. How/when used ?

1163. What happens to the recipient of services?

1164. Have all contracts been completed?

1165. Have all contract records been included in the Identity Federation project archives?

1166. Change in knowledge?

1167. Why Outsource?

1168. Was the contract type appropriate?

1169. Was the contract complete without requiring numerous changes and revisions?

1170. Change in circumstances?

1171. Are the signers the authorized officials?

1172. Have all contracts been closed?

1173. Parties: Authorized?

1174. Change in attitude or behavior?

1175. Was the contract sufficiently clear so as not to result in numerous disputes and misunderstandings?

1176. Parties: who is involved?

1177. How is the contracting office notified of the automatic contract close-out?

5.3 Project or Phase Close-Out: Identity Federation

1178. Have business partners been involved extensively, and what data was required for them?

1179. In addition to assessing whether the Identity Federation project was successful, it is equally critical to analyze why it was or was not fully successful. Are you including this?

1180. What advantages do the an individual interview have over a group meeting, and vice-versa?

1181. Who are the Identity Federation project stakeholders and what are roles and involvement?

1182. If you were the Identity Federation project sponsor, how would you determine which Identity Federation project team(s) and/or individuals deserve recognition?

1183. Who is responsible for award close-out?

1184. Planned completion date?

1185. What was expected from each stakeholder?

1186. What security considerations needed to be addressed during the procurement life cycle?

1187. What is a Risk Management Process?

1188. What was the preferred delivery mechanism?

1189. What are the mandatory communication needs for each stakeholder?

1190. Was the schedule met?

1191. What were the actual outcomes?

1192. Does the lesson describe a function that would be done differently the next time?

5.4 Lessons Learned: Identity Federation

1193. How timely was the training you received in preparation for the use of the product/service?

1194. Are new goals needed?

1195. How comprehensive was integration testing?

1196. For the next Identity Federation project, how could you improve on the way Identity Federation project was conducted?

1197. Were risks identified and mitigated?

1198. What needs to be done over or differently?

1199. Did the Identity Federation project improve the team members reputations, skills, personal development?

1200. How efficient and effective were Identity Federation project team meetings?

1201. Were the aims and objectives achieved?

1202. Did the delivered product meet the specified requirements and goals of the Identity Federation project?

1203. What were the desired outcomes?

1204. What were the success factors?

1205. Was Identity Federation project performance validated or challenged?

1206. What if anything has been lacking?

1207. Were any strategies or activities unsuccessful?

1208. Was the necessary hardware, software, accommodation etc available?

1209. What is the expected lifespan of the deliverable?

1210. Was the Identity Federation project manager sufficiently experienced, skilled, trained, supported?

1211. How useful do individuals find communications?

1212. How accurately and timely was the Risk Management Log updated or reviewed?

Index

CPSIA information can be obtained
at www.ICGtesting.com
Printed in the USA
BVHW041011200819
556236BV00011B/767/P